DISCOVER Zen

DISCOVER Zen

A Practical Guide to
Personal Serenity

david fontana PhD

CHRONICLE BOOKS
SAN FRANCISCO

Discover Zen
David Fontana

First published in the United States in 2001 by Chronicle Books LLC.

Copyright © Duncan Baird Publishers 2001
Text copyright © David Fontana 2001
Commissioned artwork copyright © Duncan Baird Publishers 2001

Conceived, created, and designed by
Duncan Baird Publishers Ltd.
Sixth Floor, Castle House
75–76 Wells Street
London W1T 3QH

Typeset in Ehrhardt MT and Rotis Sans Serif
Printed in Singapore

Library of Congress Cataloging-in-Publication Data
Fontana, David.
Discover zen : a practical guide to personal serenity /
David Fontana.
p. cm.
Includes index.
ISBN 0-8118-3196-5 (pbk.)
1. Spiritual life—Zen Buddhism. I. Title.
BQ9288 .F66 2001
294.3'444--dc21
00-050894

Commissioned illustrations: Nelly Dimitranova
Cover design: Azi Rad

Distributed in Canada by
Raincoast Books
9050 Shaughnessy Street
Vancouver, B.C. V6P 6E5

3 5 7 9 10 8 6 4

Chronicle Books LLC
85 Second Street
San Francisco, CA 94105

www.chroniclebooks.com

In Zen ... even the most mundane objects are things of wonder, if we stop to look at them, and the fact that we are alive is the biggest wonder of all.

David Fontana

CONTENTS

Introduction

Theoretical knowledge is no substitute for practical experience, and this is especially true of Zen. To penetrate deeply into Zen one needs to study with a recognized teacher, who has received the transmission from his or her own teacher, and to practise under their guidance. However, many Zen masters have eschewed the traditional view that all aspects of Zen can only be taught as an oral tradition, handed down from master to pupil. They placed no prohibition on their students circulating their sayings as written records, and many of these collections of teachings, such as the famous *Gateless Gate* (known in Japanese as the *Mumonkan*), are available to us today. In recent years many Zen contemporary masters have published their writings, which are mostly based upon compilations of their own teachings. Thus books, undeniably can encapsulate a taste of Zen.

I hope that *Discover Zen* may help to give you just such a taste by providing an introduction to Zen meditation and many of the major themes within Zen, as well as exercises to help you start Zen practice. Thus, even if you never work with a Zen teacher, this book may help you to see the world, and yourself, through Zen eyes – in a wiser, more natural, spontaneous and joyful way.

Zen is a remarkably consistent set of teachings, which testifies to its validity. But you may find that some details of theory, practice and interpretation differ from one commentator to another. Try not to become distracted by minor differences. Zen shrugs off such things, and refuses to enter into lengthy debates about them. And despite these differences, all the great Zen masters seem to have had the same vision, the same revelation of the true nature of things, the same enlightenment.

I recommend that initially you read all the way through the book to gain an overall impression of what Zen is about. The first two chapters give an outline of ideas essential to an understanding of Zen, together with some introductory exercises; and the remaining chapters look closely at the practice of Zen meditation. Spend some time reflecting upon the illustrations – they convey something of the wordless nature of Zen.

Having read the book, go back and work through each of the exercises. Don't be tempted to hurry. You may wish to stay with a particular exercise, repeating it each day, for weeks or even months before you feel ready to move on. The exercises are designed to be performed in sequence, with the lessons learned from the early ones remembered and carried with you throughout your practice. But you may well want to continue to use the earlier ones – or to return to them – even when you have moved on to the later ones.

Remember that *Discover Zen* is above all a practical guide to starting out on the Zen path. I hope you enjoy your journey.

CHAPTER 1

THE NATURE OF ZEN

We live in a supermarket of ideas, faiths, practices, theories, ideologies, and much else besides. Never in human history have there been so many movements and ideas struggling to attract our attention. Added to this, the Western world is swamped by material goods and the Western mind is dominated by the goal of material success. In all this confusion, Zen stands out as a voice of sanity. It represents a different way of seeing the world, one based upon the rediscovery of who we really are and have always been, through revealing to us our true nature.

In this chapter we set out on the Zen path. We explore what Zen is (and is not), how Zen began and its transmission through the ages. We look at Zen attitudes to life, death and rebirth, and meet the concepts of enlightenment and Nirvana (final liberation). We consider Zen and relationships, learning how to increase our compassion for others (and for all creation), and on a lighter note we discover a little-known aspect of Zen – its sense of humour.

What is Zen?

When asked "What is Zen?" a Zen master replied, "Your ordinary, everyday life." This is as good a place to start as any. Zen, like life, defies exact definition, but its essence is the experience, moment by moment, of our own existence – a natural, spontaneous encounter, unclouded by the suppositions and expectations that come between us and reality. It is, if you like, a paring down of life until we see it as it really is, free from our illusions; it is a mental divestment of ourselves until we recognize our own true nature. What, in fact, could be more ordinary?

Zen is both a practical and a spiritual path – practical because it is firmly grounded in the here and now, and spiritual because it invites us to see the essence (sometimes called "emptiness") behind the world of appearances. It is also practical because it helps us to live life spontaneously, even joyously, and spiritual because it enables us to see the sacredness of the very fact of existence. A movement (if such it can be called) within Buddhism, Zen has something to teach people from all faiths and from none. Because it is refreshingly free from dogma, Zen can help us to lead richer, less anxious, more compassionate and ultimately more effective lives.

"The Great Way is not difficult for those who have no preferences."

Huineng

As we begin to practise Zen, our mind and body learn deep relaxation and tranquillity, as well as gaining a new strength. Zen meditation allows us to see the world more clearly, to become aware of the moment-by-moment unfolding of experience and to be more conscious of the simple wonder of being alive. Zen teaches us to acknowledge our emotions and lay negativity to rest, and in time to answer fundamental questions about our own being, and about life, death and what lies beyond. As we study and practise Zen, we develop a sense of recognition, of familiarity, as if we are being reminded of something we have always known, but have long forgotten.

Zen is like a wise and compassionate friend: humorous and enigmatic, challenging yet supportive, old as the hills yet young as a new day, ever present around us yet located deep inside ourselves. That wise and compassionate friend is none other than our own true nature.

Discovering Reality Within

In the East it is said that no teachings can, by themselves, find your goal for you – indeed, it is considered foolish to suppose that they can. Teachings are only "fingers pointing at the moon", and must never be mistaken for the moon itself. Hearing about Zen is therefore no substitute for practising Zen. But although Zen teachings are only the finger, they point very clearly and directly, and the moon at which they are pointing is reality itself.

As such, they point not to some distant goal, but to yourself. Zen demonstrates that you are your own reality. Thus, Zen invites you not to find something rare and distant beyond yourself, but to uncover what is already there, to realize what you are and have always been, namely the enlightened mind (usually called the Buddha mind). How can you be anything else? How can you be other than your own true nature?

So to attain the goal and find your true nature, you need to strip away the mental "padding" from your mind, not add to it. This is beautifully demonstrated in the story of a Western scholar, who once went to a Zen master and asked to receive Zen teachings. The master invited the scholar to take tea, and proceeded to fill a cup for him. However, he did not stop once the cup was full but continued pouring until the tea overflowed. The point that the Zen master was making was that if the intellectual's mind was full of preconceptions, there was no room for Zen teachings. To be able to receive Zen wisdom, the scholar first

needed to empty the cup of his mind, rather than to pour more teachings into it.

The task of finding our own true nature, of following the finger pointing directly at reality, is emphasized in all the great spiritual traditions. Christ speaks of the Kingdom of God as being "within us" (Luke 17:21), and reminds his listeners that "you are gods" (John 10:34). Many of the great myths and folktales of the world depict the hero setting out on a quest to find a magical object – a symbol for his or her true nature – which will undo wrongs and set the world (him- or herself) to rights. What could be more important than to see where Zen is pointing, and start on our journey?

First Tastes of Zen – "Your Ordinary, Everyday Life"

If Zen is our "ordinary, everyday life", the discovery of our own true nature is literally right in front of us at each moment. Where else could it be? Life is each moment of existence as it unfolds, nothing more, nothing less. And the outer world, far from being truly "outer", is in fact experienced within the space of our own minds. This is why Zen speaks of the mind as being "sky-like", all-embracing. Without the activity of our own minds there would be for us no phenomena, no reality, no world.

The opportunity for recognizing reality, for enlightenment (there are many terms for the experience), thus presents itself in each moment. This may seem obvious if we are on a mountaintop surrounded by natural beauty instead of urban ugliness, but a fundamental principle of Zen is that each moment is precious because it is part of the priceless experience of being alive. And if our realization is genuine, it is just as likely to occur within our demanding working life as during idyllic moments on a mountaintop.

Zen asks us, in keeping with the other great traditions (the call to "Awaken!" sounds particularly loudly in Islam), to open our eyes to the fascinating business of being alive: "Don't allow your mind to become so full, so distracted that you forget who you really are," it says. And in theory, waking up to reality should be easy enough. But for the moment let us relish our first taste of Zen – the exercise opposite is designed to help us do so.

EXERCISE 1:
EXPERIENCE THE HERE AND NOW

The aim of this exercise is to increase your awareness of the present.
There is no need to adopt a special meditation posture, just sit
comfortably, with your back straight and your feet flat on the floor.

● Sitting quietly, look slowly around you wherever you happen to be.
Take in each sight and each object in turn as it presents itself to you.
Try not to label or think about what you see. Attempt simply to gain
a sense of shape, colour and presence here in space and time. Take at
least 2–3 minutes over this.

● Acknowledge that everything you see is actually taking place,
moment by moment, inside your own mind.

● Now be aware of yourself also as a presence in the here and now,
experiencing the play of your own mind, the fact that you are *alive*.

● End the exercise by offering gratitude for all the things you have
experienced, including your own mind.

How Zen Began

Zen, as a collection of teachings and a set of practices, developed in China in the sixth and seventh centuries CE. However, its roots lie partly in India and in the teachings of Siddhartha Gautama (who became known as Shakyamuni Buddha), 500 years before the birth of Christ, and partly in the Daoist religion, which flourished in China from the sixth century BCE onward. Zen probably dates back even earlier, at least in the sense that there were men and women who were following the Zen path by whatever name it was then known. For Zen, as we shall see, is grounded in a true understanding of life and of ourselves – an understanding that arises in part from the simple act of abiding calmly in the present moment and observing the nature of existence as it unfolds.

The word Zen is an abbreviation of *zenna*, the Japanese form of the Chinese *ch'an-na* (or *ch'an* for short). This, in turn, is the Chinese form of the Sanskrit *dhyana*, which means collectedness of mind, or a meditative absorption in which all dualistic, subject–object distinctions such as "I" and "you", "true" and "false" disappear. In their place there is a realization of the essential unity of all things. Formally, we date Zen from the teachings of Bodhidharma, the 28th patriarch (the 28th successor in the lineage created by the Buddha), who took his Buddhist teachings from India to China around 520CE.

Zen is described as "a special transmission outside the teachings", in that it forms no part of the orthodox canon of sutras said to enshrine the teachings of the Buddha. Some claim that Zen was given by the Buddha to Mahakashyapa, his direct disciple, in the Flower Sermon. The Buddha reportedly taught at different levels, according to the capacity of his listeners to understand and, on this occasion, instead of speaking he simply held up a flower. Only Mahakashyapa, among those present, smiled, indicating to the Buddha that he had become enlightened in that moment. Zen was therefore said to be transmitted from heart to heart, and not through written or spoken teachings. However, Zen has also produced as many texts and famous teachers as most other Buddhist traditions.

Other commentators, more prosaically, attribute Zen to Bodhidharma himself (who became the first Chinese Zen patriarch), while yet others consider it to have originated with a later Chinese patriarch Nan-ch'uan (in Japanese, Nansen). Either way, Zen established itself in China during the sixth century CE, and spread from there to Korea, reaching Japan in the seventh century, although not becoming a dominant movement within Japanese Buddhism until some 500 years later. Of the early schools of Zen, only two now survive, the Tsaotung (in Japan, Soto) and the Linchi (in Japan, Rinzai) schools, although there are several lines of transmission (that is, lineages of teachers who can trace their origins back to Bodhidharma) within both.

"Do not seek to follow in the footsteps of the ancient ones; seek what they sought."
Basho

The Tsaotung and Linchi schools were founded in China in the ninth century CE. During the Sung period (960–1126), when Zen was the dominant Buddhist practice in China, Japanese monks travelled to China to study with the most renowned Ch'an (Chinese Zen) masters. Soto Zen was established by the monk Dogen (1200–1253), after returning from a pilgrimage to China. Students of the Soto school believe that the regular practice of *zazen* (seated meditation) will lead them gradually to enlightenment. The Rinzai school, which was founded by the monk Eisei (1141–1215), who also visited China, emphasizes the study of cryptic questions and statements (koans) and teaches that enlightenment can be attained in an instant. Both the Soto and Rinzai sects are active today, and much of present Zen practice dates from the mid-seventeenth century, when a group of visiting Chinese monks reformed the whole monastic system.

GRADUAL VERSUS SUDDEN ENLIGHTENMENT

The difference between gradual and sudden enlightenment is beautifully illustrated in Zen verse by two men who were rivals to become the sixth patriarch and successor to Master Hungjen. While the favourite, Shenhsui, was the head monk at the monastery, the unlikely candidate, Huineng, was an illiterate peasant working in the kitchens, who had come to Hungjen having experienced enlightenment while listening to a reading of the *Diamond Sutra*.

Extolling the virtues of the disciplined, daily practice that leads to gradual realization, Shenhsui wrote: "The body is the Bodhi [enlightenment] tree / The mind is like a clear mirror / At all times we must wipe it clean / And must not let the dust collect."

In reply, Huineng dictated the following poem, that alludes to his own sudden illumination: "Bodhi originally has no trees / The mirror also has no stand / Buddha-nature is always clean and pure, / Where can dust alight?"

Master Hungjen chose Huineng as his successor, but fearing for the boy's safety, counselled him to flee southward. Although the defeated Shenhsui also started his own Zen school, that of Huineng eventually prevailed, becoming known as the "Southern School".

Lineages and Training

With its emphasis upon direct transmission rather than reliance upon scripture, Zen has always supported the existence of lineages – lines of succession from master to master. At each point in the succession, the master selects who is to follow him, having verified that the chosen one has achieved genuine enlightenment. Zen regards the Buddha as the first of these masters, or patriarchs, and lists many famous names, such as Asvaghosha and Nagarjuna, in the subsequent line of succession. Bodhidharma, the 28th patriarch, who took the lineage from India to China in the sixth century CE, became the first Chinese patriarch, and was followed by five others. The last of these, Huineng (Eno), left no successor, and consequently the line of patriarchs ended with him. However, the concept of lineages still remains, with several lines of succession running through the various Zen schools today.

Throughout the lineage and the subsequent lines of succession, three qualities have always been emphasized in Zen training: Great Faith, Great Courage and Great Inquiry. Great Faith refers to the belief that we all possess Buddha-nature – we are all potentially enlightened beings – and that we are all capable of revealing this nature within ourselves. Great Courage stands for the determination to practise regularly and diligently, to work hard to overcome obstacles, such as boredom and other difficulties, and to become more sensitive to the needs of others. Great Inquiry (sometimes called Great Doubt) entails seeing life as a question to which we currently do not know the answer; it means acknowledging the mystery of our own nature, and exploring this mystery tirelessly and with great resolve.

EXERCISE 2:
CULTIVATE YOUR ZEN QUALITIES

The traditional Zen qualities of Great Faith, Great Courage and Great Inquiry can be cultivated by us all and developed with practice.

- **Great Faith** Make a list of the reasons why you are drawn to Zen meditation. How and why do you believe that practising Zen can be of value to you?

- **Great Courage** Consider what kind of commitment you can make to your meditation. Perhaps start with 5 minutes each day, or if this is impossible, consider how often you can practise, and for how long. Make an initial agreement with yourself and try to stick to it.

- **Great Inquiry** Examine what puzzles you about life. What baffles you about your own identity?

- Write comments in response to these questions, and refer to them from time to time during your ongoing practice, both to remind yourself of the frame of mind with which you entered the study of Zen, and to note how your faith, courage and spirit of inquiry change and develop during the course of your practice.

Zen and Spirituality

The spirit of Zen is "your ordinary, everyday life" – the grime of the city as much as the pristine beauty of the mountain, the forest and the river. But as Zen is so grounded, so free from dogma, can it be anything more than a materialist philosophy for the here and now? Does Zen have "religious" beliefs? The answer is: not in the usual sense of the word. Zen teaches a practice and invites us to see where that practice leads, encouraging us to rely upon experience rather than upon belief. Little time is wasted in philosophical discussion and the amassing of knowledge, as illustrated by our earlier story of

ZEN AND "GOD"

Is there a "God" in Zen? As in all Buddhist traditions, Zen speaks of "beginningless time" rather than of a first moment of creation and a creator god. But if you choose to equate Nirvana with the Godhead of the monotheistic religions such as Christianity, Judaism and Islam, many Zen Buddhists would probably have no great objection, although they would insist that this absolute essence from which everything arises and of which everything is an expression lies beyond mere words.

However, in its practical way, Zen recognizes that some people need to look to something personal in their spiritual lives, and many Ch'an (Chinese Zen) masters are prepared to offer teachings in Pure Land Buddhism (see pp.128–9) to such people. This tradition teaches that Amitabha (Amidha in Japanese), the Buddha of Boundless Light, rules over the Western Paradise of *Sukhavati*, a pure land or Buddha field where those who place their trust in him are reborn.

the Western scholar, the Zen master, and the cup of overflowing tea (see pp. 14–15).

Nevertheless, Zen *is* a school of Buddhism, with monasteries, notable scholars and a reverence for Buddhist scriptures (particularly the *Heart Sutra*, which is chanted daily by Zen monks). All these factors indicate the presence of a spiritual philosophy, some aspects of which, at least, can be expressed in words. For example, Zen recognizes that there is an afterlife, albeit one no more permanent than our present existence. Zen accepts reincarnation, in this or other worlds, and affirms that final enlightenment leads to the ineffable state of Nirvana, from which there is no return to the wheel of rebirths. But Zen regards such things as relatively unimportant. In this world and in all forms of future existence, Zen focuses on the immediacy of the present moment, and it is to this present moment and to the opportunities that it offers for enlightenment that we must pay attention.

Zen, like all Buddhist schools, places great emphasis upon showing compassion toward all beings (and that includes ourselves), but self-reliance is also at the centre of its teachings. We must not wait for others to do the work for us. The Zen master can offer guidance, and can sense when a word – or even a blow – at the right moment can precipitate us into an enlightenment experience. (Like Mahakashyapa, who smiled when the Buddha held up a flower, we are said to have the capacity to become enlightened in an instant, as a result of suddenly seeing into the heart of things.) However, most of us will require a long period of Zen practice before we are ready to experience our sudden awakening. And Zen practice requires self-discipline.

There is something iron-hard about the spirit of Zen, something of enormous strength and courage. Zen abounds with stories of the hardships suffered by young men and women as they travelled for months and years in search of a teacher, and of their unshakable resolve in the face of almost overwhelming difficulties.

Equally there are stories of the unyielding sternness of certain Zen masters, who sometimes treated pupils with an indifference bordering upon cruelty. Where, we may wonder, is the compassion in such behaviour? Remember that the master asks nothing of his or her pupils that he or she has not undergone themselves; and, through an ability to identify hinderances to progress, the master always acts in a student's best interests. And a student is free to leave the master at any time and find another. In fact the master, who acts not from ego but from his or her knowledge of what the pupil needs, may suggest this course. But the pupil must have no illusions. As long as he or she remains with the master, the pupil must offer unquestioning obedience. The spirit of Zen has never claimed to be democratic!

EXERCISE 3: SEE WITH ZEN EYES

There is nothing special about the way in which Zen practitioners see the world. In fact, it is non-practitioners who view things in an extraordinary fashion, interposing labels, comparisons, concepts, judgments and so on between themselves and direct experience. This exercise shows us how to disregard such irrelevances and how to sample direct experience.

- Sit outside in a garden or a park, if possible. Adopt an upright but relaxed position and choose at random an object in front of you, such as a flower or a pine cone (or, if indoors, a vase or a bowl).

- Look at it steadily. Ignore its name and anything you know about it. Try to see it purely as a form occupying space. Each time your mind tries to think about the item, let the thought go. Note, without judgment, the object's colour, texture and shape. Take it in as it is.

- Try to concentrate on the item for 5 minutes. The object may suddenly lose all associations and becomes novel and strange (then again it may not). Either way, just engage in the act of seeing.

27

The Essence of Meditation

When they start out on the Zen path, many students show an interest in comparing Zen meditation with the practices of other traditions. And they soon discover that the fundamentals are generally the same. In all meditative traditions, attention is central to practice. The pupil concentrates unwaveringly on a point of focus – a mantra, a candle flame, a mandala, the rise and fall of the abdomen with each breath or even a blank wall. When thoughts or emotions arise, they are allowed to pass without distracting this attention. And, as the mind becomes calm, deeper levels of awareness, which are always there but usually drowned out by mental chatter, reveal themselves.

However, Zen differs from most other traditions in that ritual, worship, iconography and scripture play only a minor role. In its early history Zen regarded such things with indifference (a good example of this is the story of the Zen practitioner who burned a wooden statue of the Buddha to keep out the cold), but as time has passed a limited use of these aids to practice has been allowed.

The act of focusing attention, and how this can be carried into daily life, remains the heart of Zen practice. The student is instructed to engage the mind fully in the activity of the moment: "When washing dishes, just wash dishes. When walking, just walk," and so on. Each moment is honoured with complete attention, with the mind always present rather than distracted by thoughts. This does not mean that Zen lacks respect for thinking. In its proper place, thought is a powerful tool; and like all tools, it is there to be used. But,

according to Zen, to be of any value, thought must be focused and directed rather than scattered and confused. Nor does Zen waste words – idle chatter, particularly gossip, is always discouraged. And although it is against Zen principles to pass judgment, we can deduce that Zen would regard many other traditions as wasting time on activities that bring us no closer to enlightenment.

In short, Zen provides the bedrock of good practice upon which other traditions can base their teaching, irrespective of beliefs. The unswerving commitment to knowing our own true nature that characterizes Zen does not go amiss whatever path we choose.

The Zen State

Giving our full attention to an object or to an activity, whether in formal meditation or in everyday life, can lead to what Westerners sometimes call the "Zen state". In this frame of mind, the individual becomes so riveted, so absorbed and fully conscious, that all other things drop away. It is as if nothing outside the focus exists. Even the sense of self disappears, and there is only the act of attention, as if the mind has achieved complete unity with whatever it is doing.

The Zen state is sometimes described as blissful, as elevating the spirit, as deeply satisfying and life-enhancing, but in reality, like much else in Zen, it lies beyond words, and only those who experience it can know its true flavour. This frame of mind – comparable to the "flow"

state recognized in modern Western psychology – is familiar to the creative artist, but it can arise at any time. Most of us have probably sampled being fully focused in the present when we were engrossed in an activity, such as gardening or listening to music. But if you cannot recall having had such an experience, you can learn something of it by watching how a small child plays with a new toy or explores a novel object, remaining totally caught up in what he or she is doing.

"You should study not only that you become a mother when your child is born, but also that you become a child."

Dogen

The Zen state is created by a frame of mind rather than by anything intrinsic to the activity itself. As beginners, then, we are more likely to attain it when we are absorbed in a pleasurable activity, such as a hobby. At such times we become oblivious to everything going on around us – unaware of the passage of time, of physical sensations such as hunger or discomfort, of noises and disturbances. All existence is contained in the activity.

Rhythmic physical activities, such as walking, running or dancing, are other means through which we can reach the Zen state. Again, the mind is placed fully in the experience – in this case the movement of the body – and mind and body become unified in the present. Paradoxically, a lack of motion can also be helpful, and the diligent meditator can enter into the state at almost any time by stilling the body and allowing the mind to be fully present in this stillness. Ultimately, the advanced Zen practitioner is able to become totally focused in the present in any place, under any circumstances and in any conditions.

Life, Death and Rebirth

With its concern for living in the present, Zen does not dwell upon the afterlife, or upon issues such as rebirth. This, together with the general Buddhist refusal to discuss fundamental questions, such as the existence or non-existence of a creator god, has led to the popular (but erroneous) belief that Zen is simply a set of practices that can be used equally well by other spiritual traditions, such as Christianity. It is true that Zen has much to offer other traditions, and certainly one can practise Zen meditation without any formal allegiance to Zen.

However, it is a mistake to see Zen as anything other than primarily a movement within Buddhism, adhering to Buddhist thought, and thus neither asserting nor denying the existence of God but concerning itself more with the creative process as it unfolds in each moment. Zen can therefore be described as non-theistic.

As to death, the afterlife, and the possibilities of rebirth, Zen teaches that if you know who you are now, you will also know what part of you will survive after death. The emphasis is always upon approaching the truth through practice, rather than simply accepting dogma, either intellectually or on the basis of faith. But Zen would not have remained within Buddhism unless tacit assent was given to the Buddhist idea that life flows continuously through the pre-death and the after-death states. We live, die and live again in each moment, and we will continue to do so when we leave the physical body.

However, no Zen master would spend much time on such discussions. Instead, he or she would send us away to meditate and work on exercises such as the one opposite.

EXERCISE 4: EXPERIENCE LIFE AND DEATH IN EACH MOMENT

In Zen, each breath we take is a metaphor for our life, death and rebirth. Here, we use the essential act of breathing as a basis from which to explore the nature of our existence.

● Settle into your meditation. Then, begin to examine your breathing. A breath arises and departs, to be followed by another, and so on. Does the act of breathing live and die with each arrival and departure? Does each moment live and die in the instant it arises and passes? If these questions provoke thoughts, do they live as they arise and die as they depart? What is this "living" and "dying"?

● Now enquire about what lives in the still moment between the in-breath and the out-breath? What is it that lives in the silence between thoughts?

● Question whether life and death are opposites. Or can you see beyond these apparent opposites? Reflect how living and dying in each moment echoes the ever-changing seasons and the eternal cycle of life, death and rebirth. Try to carry into everyday life this new awareness of living, dying and living again in each moment.

Enlightenment and Nirvana

Zen meditation is associated with the achievement of enlightenment or *satori*, and perhaps even ultimate liberation – Nirvana. Given that such concepts cannot adequately be described in words, can anything useful be said about them?

Enlightenment (a glimpse into the real nature of existence) is broadly synonymous with *satori* (also known as *kensho*), a state in which the distinction between the knower and the known disappears, and the meditator experiences the unified reality underlying apparent opposites and distinctions. The Zen state (see pp.30–31) can be a fore-taste of the experience.

However, achieving *satori* does not mean that we are permanently released from our usual, deluded form of thinking. We might have many moments of *satori*, as well as many periods of doubt, before we are finally liberated. The meditator is thus counselled not to seek *satori* deliberately, nor to be excited or feel pride if it occurs. The experience arises spontaneously, and should be treated like any other, even though it undeniably marks progress on the Zen path.

Nirvana lies even further beyond description. The Buddha refused to answer questions about it, except to insist that Nirvana *is*. Although it is impossible to define Nirvana (to describe it is to limit it), its essence can be explained as that state beyond all other states and from which all other states arise. It is said that Nirvana can be experienced by the fully enlightened master here on earth, and that when he or she enters it after death, there is final freedom from the limitations of self and the cycle of death and rebirth.

EXERCISE 5: MOVE BEYOND THE SELF

One of our main obstacles to experiencing *satori* is a feeling of separateness from the world, of self-containment. This exercise will help you to realize that everything, including ourselves, is part of a universal pattern of permanent interaction.

● Sit with your back straight, in front of a window (or sit outside) and take in the view. Focus on your consciousness. Become aware that, rather than being confined to the physical limits of your body, your consciousness extends outward as far as you can see.

● Now reach out even further in your imagination. Go beyond the visible view to distant roads, hills, woodlands, cities. (It does not matter whether these imaginary scenes are accurate or not.)

● Venture further still, to the seashore, to distant lands, into space or wherever you please, while remaining aware that your consciousness is radiating outward from where you are sitting. Try to maintain this sense of mind expansion – of your unlimited self embracing all things – for as long as you can after finishing the exercise.

Zen in Relationships

Although Zen monks follow the celibate path, a number of Zen masters have been married with children. As a layman, the Zen master stands as an inspiration of the "ordinariness" of Zen, and of the fact that the Zen way is compatible with everyday life.

"The raindrops patter on the basho leaf; but these are not tears of grief; this is only the anguish of him who is listening to them."

Zen saying

One of the most interesting lay practitioners was the eighth-century Chinese master P'ang Yun, who decided at the age of 68 that it was time to die. Sitting on his meditation cushion, he told his daughter Ling-chao that he would depart when the sun reached its zenith. The girl replied that there was an eclipse that day, and called him outside to see. As soon as P'ang Yun got up to go and look, Ling-chao took his place and died. After cremating Ling-chao, the old man also died. When P'ang Yun's son Keng-huo heard of the deaths, he died too. And after cremating her son, Madame P'ang wandered off, never to be heard of again.

The behaviour of the P'ang family seems so bizarre that we may wonder what it can tell us about relationships. P'ang Yun's beautiful verse gives us a clue: "I have a boy who has no bride / I have a girl who has no groom; / Forming a happy family circle, / We speak about the Unborn." All four family members experienced the "Unborn", the true nature of life and death, and the unity that is an expression of this true nature. Thus the deaths of P'ang Yun, Ling-chao and Keng-huo were one death, while Madame P'ang's subsequent wanderings were an expression of the family's one life.

We may find all this far too extreme, but the lesson is one of connectedness. We live in the people we love and they live in us. There is a deceptively simple yet profoundly meaningful practice in Zen – try thinking "we are already connected" when you look at those whom you love, such as your parents, your partner, your children. And over time, gradually extend this practice to friends, then to acquaintances, and finally even to strangers. Emphasizing our connectedness leads us to the realization that space joins rather than separates us. We cease to regard space as a barrier, and instead experience it as an extension of ourselves, which embraces our fellow beings. The deep compassion toward others which we can acquire from this experience is one of the central features of Zen.

The Lightness of Life

Perhaps more than any other spiritual tradition, Zen releases the sense of humour that each of us has. But in Zen humour there is no mirth at the expense of others, no striving for comic effect. Instead, it arises naturally from a joyful affirmation of life, from a recognition that light and shade are two sides of the same coin. Subtly, it is also used to stir people out of their habitual way of seeing, in order to prompt the self-insight that comes from the ability to laugh at ourselves. It is not unusual for the practitioner to find him- or herself suddenly shaking with laughter (or, just as likely, sobbing) for no apparent cause.

Like all humour, that of Zen is best appreciated when we are at least slightly acquainted with the practice. Otherwise, Zen humour may seem incomprehensible. For example, what are we to make of the following story? Tokusan kept his master Ryutan up late one evening with his questions. "Why don't you go to bed?" asked Ryutan finally. Tokusan got up to leave, then said, "It's dark in the hall." "Here, take this candle," said Ryutan. Gratefully Tokusan took his master's candle. Then Ryutan leaned forward and blew it out.

How do we interpret such behaviour? Was Ryutan being unkind? Or was he trying to get Tokusan to see more deeply into his own obscurities? If the latter, and the lesson was understood, the only response could be laughter – both because this profound way of seeing is so ridiculously simple (and has always been there if only we had been able to see it) and because moments of enlightenment such as this pro-duce an immediate soaring of the spirits.

EXERCISE 6:
FIND LAUGHTER IN PRETENSION

In Zen, the ability to laugh at ourselves, and to see the humour in our fumblings and misplaced efforts, is regarded as a sign of self-insight. The following exercise is designed to help you learn to laugh at yourself without losing self-esteem.

- Think of an embarrassing experience in your life, perhaps a desire to impress that went wrong, or any other situation that dented your image of yourself. (Usually the memory of such experiences brings back the embarrassment and we try not to think about them.)

- Allow your mind to dwell lightly upon the experience. Instead of feeling anger or irritation at yourself, feel a sense of affection, as you would toward a child as he or she learns about life. Recognize that it was your own ego that caused your embarrassment, rather than the situation itself. Notice how humour arises from the difference between our pretensions (which may be grandiose) and our performance (which may be woeful).

- Laugh at the part of your ego that was wounded by the experience. Try to see this aspect of your ego for what it is and understand where it comes from within yourself. Then gently let it go.

CHAPTER 2

THE ZEN VISION

A puzzled monk once challenged Zen master Fuketsu: "You say truth can be expressed without speaking, and without keeping silent. How can this be?" Fuketsu answered, "In southern China in the spring, when I was only a lad, ah! how birds sang among the blossoms!" Like so many of the sayings of the Zen masters, Fuketsu's answer is a subject for meditation. These wise words settle into the unconscious, reminding us at a subtle level of the real meaning of truth, the Zen vision, that is expressed all around us in the beauties of nature and in the mind of a child.

This chapter focuses on Zen sources of inspiration, and art forms (which are themselves types of meditation). We explore the Zen link with nature and gardens; we learn about the formal arts of flower-arranging and tea-making; we consider Zen symbolism; and we look at Zen painting and poetry and how each one of these can help us to reconnect with that part of ourselves whose wisdom lies beyond words.

Zen and Nature

Owing partly to the formative influence of Daoism, the Zen tradition embraces a keen appreciation of nature and of the natural world. In Zen, we are encouraged to experience the changing face of nature at first hand as often as possible. Enjoying the sensation of the sun on our body or the wind in our hair helps us to feel truly alive.

"The almighty sky does not hinder white clouds in their flight."
Ryokan

The Zen practitioner sees him or herself as part of nature, playing an integral role in the remarkable phenomena of creation and growth – one of the main reasons why followers often prefer to meditate outside. The natural world also provides a rich source of inspirational aids to practice. For example, a lofty mountain is regarded as a particularly good focus to help the mind realize its potential, as is running water, which encapsulates the eternal movement and flow of all things. In fact, the ability of water to find its way around obstacles, and to become in turn a rushing torrent, then a tranquil lake, is often seen as analogous to the action of the enlightened mind.

As the practice of Zen meditation progresses, so the meditator gains more control, not only over the mind but also over the body. Thus he or she remains relaxed and at peace during long periods of sitting, and becomes immune to many of the rigours of climate encountered while practising outside. The less we feel in conflict with the elements and the less we strive compulsively to change things so that they accord with our own preferences, the more we can live at peace with the world.

EXERCISE 7:
DISCOVER HARMONY IN ALL THINGS

In Zen, harmony stems from unity – each aspect of the whole relating smoothly to every other part. By drawing your attention to imbalances in your body, this exercise suggests how to redress them so that you can apply the same principles to all aspects of your life.

- Focus on the way you move and carry out simple tasks. Notice any awkwardness or unnecessary effort in acts such as sitting and standing. Is one part of your body feeling out of kilter with the others? If so, try to correct the disparity. For example, if you are right-handed, use the left side of your body as much as you can today, or vice versa.

- Try to slow down everything you do, and be conscious of moving easily through space. Listen to your own speech. Is it jerky or hurried or hesitant? Aim to do everything smoothly and gracefully.

- At the end of the exercise review what you have learned about yourself, and try to carry the lessons into daily life.

The Zen Garden

Buddhism reached Japan in the sixth century CE, and with the founding of the first monasteries there was a need to restore and cultivate the land that had been enclosed and disturbed by building. Thus the first landscaped monastery gardens were created. In keeping with Buddhist teachings, these gardens attempted to capture the beauty of natural scenery while maintaining an emphasis on simplicity.

However, when Zen was introduced to Japan in the twelfth and early thirteenth centuries, this simplicity was taken to extremes. Many Zen gardens were composed only of rocks, moss and carefully raked

MAKE YOUR OWN MINIATURE ZEN GARDEN

Although many people who live in cities have no garden, a number of us have a balcony or access to a roof terrace, where we can capture the essence of a Zen garden by creating our own miniature version in a container.

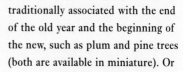

Choose a selection of small flowers, shrubs and dwarf trees and place them in a window box or other suitable receptacle. Select plants that will flourish in your climate. If you live in a temperate zone, you may wish to feature plants which, in Japan, are traditionally associated with the end of the old year and the beginning of the new, such as plum and pine trees (both are available in miniature). Or if you live in hot, semi-arid conditions, you can use flowering, succulent plants, such as cacti, as a basis for your garden.

Even if you have no outside space you can still make a tiny indoor Zen garden, using, for example, a large, shallow container in which you arrange some moss and stones around a bonsai tree.

patterns in sand, the aim being not only to symbolize aspects of nature, but also to arouse in the observer an awareness of the hidden essence that underlay the outward appearance of the garden. For example, ripples raked in the sand and carefully directed around outcrops of rock represent the ability of water to flow around obstacles, but at a deeper level they represent the way in which the mind reflects pure reality before it becomes distracted and sidetracked by intrusive thoughts. Such a garden can become a focus for meditation rather than simply a pleasant environment. The Zen practitioner concentrates on the silent garden, calming his or her mind and opening him- or herself up to the profound, wordless truth that is enshrined in all that he or she sees.

Raking and tending the monastery garden also becomes a meditation for the monks. The ripples in the sand are rearranged frequently with a wooden rake, not only denoting the impermanence of all created things, but also reflecting the movement of the monk's own mind as he rakes. The garden symbolizes Zen's rejection of over-elaborateness, and its recognition that the ultimate truth can be identified all around us, even in the sand and stones beneath our feet.

Outside the monasteries, Zen gardens adhere to the same principles. The garden is a teaching aid, a way of enabling the householder and the visitor to obtain insights into the enlightened state of his or her own mind. At each turn of the path there is harmony, an exquisite yet breathtakingly simple re-creation of the endless vistas of nature within a small space – moments of joy at, for example, the natural sculpture of the rocks, each placed to perfection, trees and passing clouds reflected in still waters, bridges over streams symbolizing the moment when the mind gains new insights, and so on.

Many practitioners like to design at least part of their own garden according to Zen principles. Why not set aside a small area in which to make your own Zen garden? The starting point is always nature itself. Let yourself be drawn to a particular rock or stone, to a group of trees or shrubs, to hillocks and undulations, to a natural hollow that

suggests a shady pool. Then choose this particular spot for open-air meditation, and over the days and perhaps weeks, wait patiently until (working always with nature) you come to know exactly which features you should have in your garden.

As all things are sacred in Zen, and nothing is too humble, you may wish to include such items as stones, the fallen branches of trees, feathers, perhaps even the bones or the skull of a small animal – these are just as important to the garden as trees, plants and flowers. If you have a water feature, remember to take special care in the placement of any objects that are reflected in its surface.

Zen and Flower Arrangement

In Zen, painting and gardening do not stop at appearances but are entered into as a means of looking more deeply into the mystery of existence. Equally, the ancient art of flower arrangement does not stop at decoration. The way in which flowers are selected, handled and placed in the vase are all expressions of the arranger's relationship with nature and with the spiritual essence of which nature is a manifestation. A Zen master may specialize in flower arrangement, just as he or she may specialize in the tea ceremony, or in one of the other meditative activities through which Zen is clearly expressed.

One of the best accounts of an apprenticeship in flower arrangement is given by Gustie Herrigel (*Zen in the Art of Flower Arrangement*), who spent six years studying under Master Bokuyo Tokeda in Japan. Herrigel speaks of the care with which the master untied the bundle of willow branches to be used in her first lesson ("no pulling or cutting, no impatience, no disorder"), the silence in which the work took place, the precise movements of the master's hands, the total concentration upon the task itself. Once the branches were set out on the table together with the vase, there followed a contemplative examination of each of them, as there "arose before the master's eye the image ... to be put together".

Herrigel reports that throughout her years of study, the master always applied the same unhurried attention to detail, the same respect for the plants and other materials used, and the same meditative concentration. And, although Zen flower arrangement is a matter of spontaneous expression, there are careful rules and techniques which must be followed, the basic principles of which we can all adopt when we place flowers in a vase (see box, below).

THE PRINCIPLE OF THREE

Zen flower arrangement has regard for the Zen "Principle of Three", which divides the universe into three realms: Heaven, Earth and the human world (although in essence all three are one). After cutting a Y-shaped fork from pliable wood and wedging it horizontally an inch down in the mouth of the vase to provide support, three main branches, carefully selected for their ability to be gently stroked and persuaded into the required shapes, are inserted. Following the "Principle of Three", the branches, each with its distinctive shape, represent Heaven, Earth and humankind (*shin*, *gyo* and *so*) respectively.

The stems are bunched together as they are put into the vase, so that the effect is of a single branch unfolding into a triangular shape (bonsai trees are also pruned to follow this form).

Zen and the Seasons

With its profound awareness of nature, Zen is very much in harmony with changes in the seasons, regarding the common tendency to grumble at the weather as a sign of great mental immaturity. As we cannot change the weather and the coming and going of the seasons, our response should be one of acceptance – indeed of joy – toward whatever nature has to offer.

In summer, the land is rich and fertile, bright with flowers and foliage. Autumn brings a deepening of colours, the ripening of crops, and a hint of the cold winds to come. Winter is frugal and sombre, with bare branches against a heavy sky, and a hard frost in the mornings. Spring sees life return to the land, a softening of winter's austerity, and a foretaste of the warmth and gold of summer. According to Zen, all are gifts freely given, to be received with gratitude.

The Zen response to the seasons is an example of how harmony arises naturally once we recognize the essential unity of all things. The Zen practitioner does not feel him- or herself to be at odds with the rain or the cold of winter or the heat of the summer sun, because he or she recognizes our deep connection with them. Not only does nature, in all its moods, give and sustain life, but it also shows us the impermanence of all created things, the constant cycle of growth, decay and regrowth in all natural phenomena, thus mirroring the cycle of human existence from birth to death and rebirth.

This feeling of harmony and unity with the seasons finds expression in Zen art and poetry, which we come to later in the book, and in the art of flower arrangement, which we have just discussed.

EXERCISE 8: TUNE IN TO THE SEASONS

You can help yourself to tune in to the cycle of the seasons by making your own flower arrangement that reflects the changes as they occur. Start with the "Principle of Three" (see p.49), and then add extra branches, leaves and flowers, in keeping with the current season.

- Try to feel a sense of connection between yourself and the arrangement, as if you are sharing a celebration of the natural world. Place each branch so that it spreads out freely, but take care not to obscure any flowers. Keep the arrangement open – it should express space as well as form.

- Although the act of flower arranging is a meditation in itself, you can also use the end product as a meditative focus. For example, if you have made a spring arrangement, meditate on the new life that is blossoming around you in the gardens, parks and countryside; if it is autumn, reflect on the bounty of Nature's gifts, and so on. Try to be more aware of the seasons and tune in to nature's eternal cycle.

The Spirit of Place

Buddhism sometimes uses the term "spirit of place" to refer to the qualities and the atmosphere possessed by a particular site or area. Zen emphasizes the influence that this spirit of place can have upon individuals, and the Zen practitioner would deplore the kind of environments in which most of us live and work, robbed as they are of any sense of order, character and even humanity. Before interfering in any way with nature (whether by building a house or removing a tree), the Zen practitioner will meditate upon the proposed change, and take no action until he or she intuitively knows that it will not interfere with the spirit of place. Such careful consideration ensures that, when a house is constructed, the exterior will blend in with the scenery, or when a tree is felled this will not cause disharmony.

ZEN AND FENG SHUI

Zen has certain affinities with the art of *feng shui* – a system of influences that are considered when siting buildings – which was first developed in China more than 2,000 years ago. Feng shui (literally meaning "wind and water") seeks to balance the five elements that are recognized in early Chinese science: earth, fire, metal, water and wood, and the two primary creative forces, *yin* and *yang* (female and male; outer and inner; form and emptiness). These five elements and two forces were believed to interact throughout nature, and to render some places more auspicious than others for human habitation.

Inside a house or a temple the same interactions were thought to take place, making the choice and placement of each item of furniture of great importance to the wellbeing of the people who lived and worshipped there.

Inside the house, the same attention that is given to a Zen garden will be given to harmonizing the furnishings and decoration and, as with the garden, concern will be shown for the principles found in nature, so that the building can develop its own spirit of place.

Zen gardens and interiors are characterized by simplicity, spareness, tranquillity, naturalness and a total absence of extraneous features. To some they may look frugal, even austere, but the greater our awareness of Zen, the more we can appreciate them for the way in which they harmonize space and emptiness, movement and stillness. In contemplating Zen gardens and interiors, the mind finds itself entering into this harmony, so that we come to recognize as illusory the habitual distinction that we draw between outer and inner worlds.

Zen in the Art of Tea-making

Few things seem stranger to Westerners than the notion that making a cup of tea can become a meditation. But any activity carried out with the mind properly focused can be a meditation, and acts of making and serving tea are seen by Zen as particularly appropriate for promoting concentration.

The keynotes of the ceremony are attention and simplicity – anything superfluous is stripped away. As with all Zen interiors, the setting is free from extraneous furniture or clutter. The atmosphere is harmonious, the light restful, the air scented with incense. Ideally the teacups are handmade, and the napkins and the tea-maker's kimono are pristine in their cleanliness. The only sounds are the bubbling of the boiling water followed by the gentle flow of the tea into the cups. By focusing upon each detail of the ceremony, the onlooker participates fully in the meditation, and sometimes he or she has a moment of insight when these soft sounds and the silence surrounding them, together with the graceful movements of the tea-maker and the stillness in the room, coalesce into a single experience.

"The essence of the Tea Way:
To boil the water,
To stir the tea and
To drink it – nothing else!
This is worth knowing."
Rikyu

Attended to in the right frame of mind, the tea ceremony is not only a profound meditative experience, but also an example of how the most apparently mundane actions can become sacred. It would be unrealistic to suggest that we should approach all our daily tasks in this manner, but we can try to bring to them something of the careful attention and unhurried grace that the tea ceremony demonstrates.

EXERCISE 9:
UNDERSTAND FORM AND EMPTINESS

Zen places great emphasis upon form and emptiness, seeing them not as opposites, but as qualities that intimately depend on each other. This exercise will help you understand this fundamental Zen concept.

- Place a teacup on the table in front of you, and look down at it. Notice the form of the cup, and the space into which the tea is poured. Focus upon the relationship between them. Would the cup be a cup without both its outer form and its inner space? Now concentrate on the space outside the cup. Could the cup exist without this space, without this emptiness?

- When you have answered these questions, put them to one side. Now focus upon the direct experience of emptiness-form-emptiness. Allow the wordless experience to fill your mind.

- Finally, look around the room and experience the subtle interplay between form and emptiness in everything you see.

The Symbols of Zen

There is a Zen saying that "everything is symbolic, yet there is no difference between the symbol and the thing symbolized." Like so much in Zen, at first sight this saying appears paradoxical. Symbols, by definition, represent something other than themselves, yet Zen seems to be telling us that the symbol and the thing it represents are one and the same. How then do we begin to comprehend such an apparent contradiction?

We can try approaching the paradox intellectually. We can regard everything as symbolic, that is, not ultimately real in itself, so that we

ZEN ANIMALS AND FIGURES

Animals feature frequently in Zen symbolism. The tiger often stands for the teacher and the fierceness that is needed to overcome the recalcitrant mind, while monkeys represent greed, and rabbits and frogs the unthinking behaviour of most men and women.

The carp – a popular image in Zen temples – is regarded as a positive symbol. With its ability to leap in and out of water, the fish represents the freedom of the enlightened mind, and serves as a reminder that we can all realize our own true nature through dedicated Zen practice.

Human figures sometimes also serve as symbols. In Ch'an (Chinese Zen) Ksitigarbha is the Buddha who opens the gates of hell and rescues suffering souls; Kwan Yin is the female Bodhisattva of Compassion, while the large, round belly of Pu-te (a familiar figure, often equated in the minds of non-Buddhists with the historical Buddha) stands for the grounding, the "settling into the self", which meditators gain as their practice progresses.

see the thing symbolized as no more real than the symbol. Alternatively, we can choose to consider both the thing symbolized and the symbol as manifestations of the one underlying reality, and therefore as not distinct from each other. However, such answers do not embody the full meaning of the paradox, which can only be grasped intuitively, and by much reflection in the context of a growing understanding of Zen. The result is a sudden insight, a feeling of knowing that cannot be put into words, which produces another paradox – we *know*, yet we do not know exactly what it is that we know.

At this stage we may feel that we will never understand Zen symbolism. Nevertheless, it is worth persevering, as working with the symbols themselves is important. The Swiss psychoanalyst Carl Jung pointed out that genuine symbols differ from such things as logos in that symbols are not contrived by the conscious mind, but arise spontaneously from the unconscious. They are therefore universal and can be used as keys to help unlock the unconscious mind.

Seen through the eyes of Zen, the world is full of symbols, and because Zen is so grounded in reality, the natural world is a major source of them. As well as trees and plants (see p.44), fruit is rich in symbolism. Pomegranates and oranges represent fertility and abundance, while cherries signify the destiny that awaits a warrior.

Even the humble possessions of a monk have significance. The robe (traditionally black in Japanese Zen, sometimes brown in Chinese Ch'an) and the bowl represent not only the necessities of physical life, but also the transmission of Zen teachings, which are all we need for true understanding. Sandals, the staff, the path and the journey all signify progress toward enlightenment, and also remind us to stay alert in case we miss what we are seeking, as echoed in the Zen saying, "I thought I had a long way to go until I looked back and saw that I had passed my destination many years before." Other common Zen symbols include incense, which gives fragrance to others while consuming itself – signifying selflessness; the candle flame, representing wisdom; and water, which in adapting itself to all situations denotes flexibility as well as purity.

But of all symbols, it is the circle that is most associated with Zen, representing as it does both outer and inner, no beginning and no end, completion. The Zen scholar D.T. Suzuki spoke of the practitioner following a long pathway around the circumference of a circle, which eventually leads back to the starting point, to him- or herself, yet to a self with a difference, for now he or she has had the experience of the journey and is changed from the person he or she once was. The self is thus both the reason for the journey and the goal of the journey, both the path and the fruit of the path, both the question and the answer. And by "self" Zen means self-knowing, the recognition of our essential nature, which is ultimately identified with "emptiness", the infinite potential, from which all things arise.

Zen and the Art of Painting

Zen painting is spontaneous and effortless, but it requires years of practice and a mastery of technique. Zen artists have adopted the six principles of Chinese painting, which were laid down more than 1,500 years ago. In brief they are these: a painting must have life and variety; the brush should be used in a controlled manner; the subject of the painting should capture the essence rather than the actuality of a subject but should be recognizable; the major brush strokes should be made in black, with colour used carefully; the painting should be positioned so that two thirds of the paper is left unpainted; and the artist should copy the work of a master many times.

"I express my mind using a brush instead of my tongue, and you seize my meaning hearing my words with your eyes."
Ch'an (Chinese Zen) master

The brush is held between the first two fingers and is steadied with the thumb. Each stroke begins and ends with the brush in an upright position. The first step is to practise a single stroke until the master deems it perfect. Several strokes are then put together as an exercise. Next the artist copies the work of a master until the copy, too, is perfected. Only then are more difficult compositions attempted, with copying again serving as the main aid to learning.

Typically, there is no focal point in a composition. The viewer's eyes should travel visually through the scenery, discovering vistas as if on a real journey. Tiny human figures emphasize the vastness of nature and distance is conveyed vertically rather than by perspective. Sometimes landscapes symbolize the human form, containing water (blood), trees (bones), mountains (the body) and clouds (the spirit).

EXERCISE 10: EXPRESS "CATNESS" OF CAT, "TREENESS" OF TREE

A Zen painting embodies the essence of the object being represented. In this exercise you attempt to capture this essence yourself. You will need a brush (cut to a chisel-like point) and some rice or bamboo paper.

- Load the brush with black ink or paint. Close your eyes and picture a cat. What is it that makes it a cat? The arch of the back? the eyes? the claws? – or some other indefinable quality? When the image is clear in your mind, open your eyes and convey it to paper, with a few swift brush strokes. Then repeat the same exercise with a tree.

- Now study your paintings. Have you managed to capture the "catness" of cat and the "treeness" of tree? If not, look at the illustrations above and below and try to identify what it is that makes them successful. Then copy them.

Capturing the Essence in Words

Just as the Zen painter captures the essence of an
object in paint, so the Zen poet encapsulates it in words.
The result is the *haiku*, a three-line, typically seventeen-
syllable verse, the brevity of which is matched only by its ability to arouse in the reader a sense of recognition, as if he or
she has actually become the poet. Here is a typical *haiku*,
written in the eighteenth century by Yosa Buson: "Autumn evening –
/ there's joy also / in loneliness." This poem about the passing of the
seasons, captures the reflective melancholy that such transience
evokes. The verse renders, in simple purity, a sudden sense of existing,
of capturing the exact mood and feel of the experience. It also alludes
to the stillness of an autumn evening, and to the quiet acceptance of
loneliness. The reader either instinctively understands or completely
misses these things in the immediacy of a first reading.

No literature compares with the *haiku* in conveying emotions in
a few words. In the following eighteenth-century verse we can share
the aching sense of loss felt by Chiyo-jo at the death of her small
son: "The little dragon-fly hunter - / how far, I wonder, / has
he gone today?" There are also moments of insight which
provide a fleeting glimpse of completeness, as in this
seventeenth-century example by Basho: "Very brief: / gleam
of blossoms in the treetops / on a moonlit night." Basho uses the
image of blossoms again, this time to convey the spiritual longing
that is so much a part of Zen: "More than ever I want to see / in
these blossoms at dawn / the god's face."

EXERCISE 11: COMPOSE A HAIKU

Like the Zen painter, the *haiku* poet studies with a master. But we all
have *haiku* in us, and if a composition presents itself it may reveal the
progress we have made to date in our practice.

● Find a restful place, preferably outside – *haiku* are best written close
to nature. Enter a calm, meditative state of mind. Be aware of the
season, the feeling of warmth or cold on your body, the passing
of time and yet the timelessness of each moment. Notice your
surroundings: trees, flowers, the wind in the branches. Think
about your life, your memories and hopes, and your feelings. Just
keep your present awareness and see what arises.

● Remember a *haiku* usually has 17 syllables (although in translation
from the Japanese, syllables may be lost or gained). However, for
now, just try to express your awareness of the moment in 8–12
words. Once you have written the *haiku*, do not try to improve it.
Leave it, just as it is. If nothing comes, do not be dismayed. If you
persevere, your *haiku* will present itself at the right time – suddenly
and ready-made, as if it has always existed.

CHAPTER 3

ENTERING THE PATH

*T*o the onlooker, a person meditating appears to be doing nothing. There is the story of a young novice monk, who at the end of his first meditation session turned to his senior and enquired eagerly as to what happened next. The older man looked at him and raised his eyebrows in amazement, "What happens next? This is it." Just so – in Zen we meditate because, in Master Dogen's words, that is what Buddhas do. But of course, the young monk had a point. As meditation practice develops, deeper levels of awareness reveal themselves. The elderly monk had a point too. Nothing is required of us in meditation beyond patience, and the ability to focus our mind and keep it clear of distractions.

In this chapter we consider the practical aspects of meditation, such as how and where to sit, and what to wear. We also explore Zen ways to help focus our minds through the practice of mindfulness, *kinhin* (walking meditation) and t'ai chi, as well as how to deal with both physical and mental obstacles.

Starting Formal Meditation

Meditation, in the sense of focused awareness upon the activity in hand and a refusal to be distracted by extraneous thoughts or events, is something that can be practised at any time in daily life. However, if we wish to make genuine progress, it is best to allocate a specific period for undertaking formal sitting meditation, once or twice a day.

Before you commit yourself to a routine, it is a good idea to decide how formal meditation will fit into your life. It is no use setting yourself overly-ambitious targets only to abandon them as unsustainable. Five minutes per day, every day, are better than an hour per day which tails off into nothing once your initial enthusiasm wanes. Moreover, an hour a day is not only difficult to arrange, taking into consideration other commitments (particularly if you have a demanding job, a partner or young children), it is also asking too much of most beginners. When starting meditation the mind is typically very wayward, and if we spend an hour lost in distracting thought, we are likely to become quickly discouraged.

Begin by deciding on the best time of day for your meditation. Research has shown that three quarters of meditators prefer the early morning, while the rest favour the evening, just prior to going to bed – but choose whenever is right for you. Pick a time when you are relaxed and unlikely to be interrupted, and attempt to keep to this same schedule daily, as routine helps the mind turn toward meditation when the set time arrives.

Try to sit in the same place for each session, whether inside or outside. Your chosen spot is important – like the time of day, it should help to draw your mind to meditation. While a special meditation room would be ideal, few of us have sufficient space for this, so a spare room or even the corner of a bedroom will do. The crucial thing is that you can sit facing a blank wall or a closed cupboard door. You can set an alarm or timer to let you know when the meditation period is completed, and it is helpful to keep a small bell which you can ring at both the start and finish of the session, as a further aid to practice (see pp.74–7).

"The Great Path has no gate, thousands of roads enter it. When one passes through this gateless gate, One walks freely between heaven and earth."
Mumon

How to Sit

The way in which we sit during *zazen* – the seated form of Zen meditation – is absolutely vital to the practice. The postures which are taught today are the same as those that were used by the early masters thousands of years ago. It is therefore worth spending a little time considering these tried-and-tested positions to learn how to adopt them correctly.

As a general rule you should always sit firmly rooted to the ground, and keep your back and head straight. If at first the positions feel uncomfortable, remember that most Westerners are used to sitting on soft chairs. With patience and practice the postures *will* become comfortable and you may even find that sitting on chairs starts to feel unnatural.

For many people the popular image of a meditator is of someone sitting cross-legged and there are many postures which are variations on this position. To assume any cross-legged posture correctly you will need to sit on a hard cushion, which should be firm enough to raise your buttocks four inches (10 cm) from the ground. Make sure that you keep your back straight as this encourages the spine to support the entire weight of the upper body. For all postures your hands should rest gently in your lap, palms upward, your left hand on top of your right hand. The tips of your thumbs should lightly touch.

Probably the best-known posture in the West (but also one of the most difficult to attain and hold) is the Lotus position. Work toward achieving the full Lotus position by beginning with the Quarter Lotus (see illustration in the exercise, opposite). Sitting cross-legged on your

EXERCISE 12: JUST SIT AND BREATHE

Zen meditation is sometimes described as "just sitting", which implies that we do not have to make an effort to do much else. Often, it is when we are simply sitting and paying attention to our breath that our true nature reveals itself.

- Sit on your cushion and take up your meditation posture (suggested positions are given in the main text) and, when you are comfortable, turn your attention to your breathing. Focus upon the coolness of the air as you breathe it in through your nose, and upon its warmth as you exhale it through your nostrils. Notice the quite subtle but unmistakable sensations.

- When thoughts come to your mind, try to let them pass in to and out of awareness without distracting your attention. But if your mind does wander, bring it gently back to focus on your breath. Even if your mind constantly strays, remember that this waywardness is precisely the reason why we need to meditate. With practice, your mind will come increasingly under control.

- Keep up the practice for 5 minutes, and then end by gently swaying your body from side to side 2–3 times.

cushion, draw in your left heel until it is touching the perineum. Slide forward until you are almost sitting on the heel, then cross your right leg over the left one. If you find this position uncomfortable because it puts too much pressure on your legs and feet, try sitting on a low stool that slopes gently downward from back to front.

When you have mastered the Quarter Lotus, progress to the Half Lotus. For this posture place your left foot and leg on your right thigh and tuck your right leg and foot underneath. And once you have become more supple and you feel comfortable in the Half Lotus position, you can try the Full Lotus posture. This time cross your legs so that your right leg and foot rest on your left thigh and your left foot and leg are on your right thigh.

If you are unable to sit on the floor for any reason, you can meditate sitting in a chair. Be sure to keep your head straight and your neck and back upright and place your feet flat on the floor.

Whether you sit in a chair or on the floor, take some time to get your position right. Your body should feel comfortable and well-balanced: check for areas of tension and try to relax them (direct your breath into "tight spots" and breathe them free). Some teachers recommend rocking gently a few times from side to side to complete the process of settling yourself.

ARE YOU SITTING COMFORTABLY?

Meditation is not meant to be a trial of endurance. It does strengthen the will, but this does not happen overnight. Forcing yourself to endure physical pain and discomfort when you already have enough to contend with at mental and emotional levels is a sure way of bringing your interest in Zen meditation to a premature end. A few simple rules should ensure this need not happen.

Always limit the length of time you sit. Start with 5 minutes or so, and gradually lengthen the sessions as you become more experienced. Even when your practice is well-developed, do not sit for too long. Thirty minutes is the usual limit in Zen, after which time you should undertake stretching and walking exercise for 10 minutes. You can then sit again if you wish.

If you do experience slight discomfort, try to resist dealing with it straight away. Once you familiarize yourself with the distracting physical sensation, you may find that it is less powerful than you first thought. Sit with it for a while, keeping your attention on your breathing, and you may find that the discomfort diminishes or even disappears.

As you meditate look straight ahead, or slightly downward. It is customary to keep your eyes slightly open, as Zen does not encourage complete withdrawal from the world, but in the early days of practice you may find it easier to concentrate if you close them.

Keep monitoring your position during meditation. For example, you may find that your shoulders and head have a tendency to slump forward. If this happens, gently straighten yourself up again. It may help to imagine a thin thread pulling you up by the crown of your head. Otherwise, keep any movement to a minimum. Do not be tempted to squirm on your seat in search of a more comfortable position – the stiller the body, the stiller the mind is likely to be.

Posture and Practice

In Zen meditation practitioners are encouraged to pay attention to two things: *shi*, which means "stopping" (the cessation of both physical and mental movement), and *kan*, meaning "objective view" (the objective view that results from *shi*, and allows everything to be seen just as it is).

"When we do zazen, the quality of our calm, steady serene sitting is the quality of the immense activity of being itself."
S. Suzuki

Shi is impossible without the good meditation posture that helps the mind to remain alert and the body to relax. Many of us find it uncomfortable to sit in one position for extended periods, but with practice you will eventually be able to sustain your meditation posture for long periods with great ease. It is worth remembering that provided you hold your back straight, your body can remain unsupported without discomfort, and your breathing will remain deep and unrestricted.

In Zen monasteries, the head monk or nun walks along the row of meditators carrying a *keisaku*, a long flat stick which is used to strike the shoulders of anyone found dozing or slumping. Wielded expertly, the *keisaku* causes no damage or great pain, but its loud thwack and attendant tingling sensation quickly remind the practitioner of the importance of *shi*. If a monk or nun feels drowsy or has a wandering mind, he or she will voluntarily bend forward when the *keisaku* approaches. Of course, the head monk or nun who uses the stick is regarded as showing great compassion!

Kan is said to be present at all times in the mind, but hidden from view by the movement of thoughts. Once we are able to hold our attention on our breath (see p.69), our first experience of *kan* is often an awareness of the coming and going of the breath. Something that is taken for granted becomes the whole of awareness – a gentle, caressing touch full of mystery and beauty. There is a sense of fullness (or form) as the breath enters the body, and emptiness as it leaves. Eventually, you may even experience the sensation that you are "being breathed" rather than actively breathing.

As your practice develops, you may also become aware of your own sense of presence, of your form occupying space. Your body may seem empty, or as if transparent; or all sensation may disappear, as if your physical shell has fallen away. Or perhaps your body may seem so light that it appears to levitate, or so heavy that it is immoveable. It is important not to regard such *kan* experiences as a source of pride or a result of your own efforts. Remember, they arise of their own accord once the mind becomes still.

Rituals and Robes

In spite of its uncomplicated approach to meditation, Zen sometimes makes extensive use of ritual. The purpose behind this ritual is not to please deities or Celestial Buddhas, but to act as a sign of respect for the teachers, as a reminder of your practice, as an aid to mindfulness and self-awareness, and as a help in focusing and calming the mind.

In Japanese monasteries and retreats there is much formality, with many directives on how to behave at meal times, how to conduct yourself during the day, how to walk, how to sit, and how to enter and leave the meditation hall. There is much prostrating yourself (in front of

WHAT TO WEAR FOR MEDITATION

Your choice of clothes can be a useful aid to practice. If possible keep some garments purely for meditation – perhaps a robe or a loose top and trousers, such as a tracksuit – and change into them before you begin sitting. Whatever you wear should be comfortable, and of a colour appropriate to meditation. You could follow the example of Zen monks, who usually wear black or dark brown; or you could choose maroon or saffron – the colours worn by other Buddhist monks. By experimenting with different colours you can discover what seems appropriate for you. But try to avoid bright shades, which are on the whole too distracting.

When meditating alone some practitioners prefer to sit naked, which they feel symbolizes the simplicity and naturalness of Zen. Although at first the idea of sitting without clothes may seem strange, it is perhaps worth trying. Nudity can help us to recognize how, when in deep meditation, our bodies are able to adapt with equanimity to wide variations in temperature.

your teacher), much bowing (to your meditation cushion), and much ringing of bells (at the beginning and end of meditation sessions).

The day starts with a ceremony involving both chanting and the recitation of sutras, in particular the *Heart Sutra*, with its repeated message that form is emptiness and emptiness is form. There may also be three formal bows or prostrations, paying respect in turn to the Buddha, to the Dharma (ultimate reality and the path to this reality) and to the Sangha (teachers and fellow practitioners), bows which are also a mark of respect to your own potentially enlightened mind (Buddha nature).

If, like many meditators, you are practising alone or with a small group, you may find it helpful to use simple rituals at the start and end

of each session. These may consist of practices which you have learned on retreats or from recognized Zen teachers, or they may be ones you devise for yourself (see exercise, opposite). However, given that you are practising Zen, it is important that you ensure that all rituals you use are in keeping with the true spirit of Zen.

As iconography has recently become more accepted by Zen, setting the scene using incense, pictures or *rupas* (small brass, wooden or resin statues of respected Buddhist figures) or devotional statuettes from your own religious tradition, may also help to turn your mind to meditation. You should treat such pictures, *rupas* and figurines with respect, but bear in mind too that they are there to offer you support, in much the same way as friends.

It should, of course, be stressed that rituals, including the wearing of special clothing, are only there to help practitioners to settle into the right state of mind for meditation, and are not in themselves an essential part of the practice. In fact, some Western meditation groups have dispensed with rituals altogether, while others use them only on special occasions.

Like so much else in Zen, rituals should be undertaken with an open mind, and you should monitor closely the effect that they have upon your ability to practise and the progress that you make. Zen does not ask for blind obedience, but it does require the mind to be disciplined. If by creating a set of outer rituals we can encourage the development of inner discipline, then Zen would regard it as foolish not to make use of them.

EXERCISE 13: CREATE A ZEN RITUAL

When devising your own ritual, you might like to incorporate some or all of the traditional elements suggested below – they are all tried-and-tested ways to help you to focus on your practice.

- Ring a bell three times at the beginning of the session and once at the end. Listen to the sound as it fades softly away, taking the mind deeper into itself at the beginning of the session and bringing it back to focus on everyday life at the end.

- Before you sit, give three respectful bows, then turn and bow to your cushion – after all, it is aiding you with your practice.

- Prior to ending your session, say a prayer. If you are a Buddhist, you may wish to recite: "I take refuge in the Buddha, the Dharma and the Sangha" several times; if you are a Christian you might prefer to put your trust in the Holy Trinity; other religious paths will suggest other wording. And if you belong to no particular religion at all, you might like to address your petitions to Wisdom, Love and Peace, or any other qualities that bring tranquillity to the spirit.

Meeting Your Own Mind

We often say that indecisive people appear not to know their own minds, but the same is true for most of the rest of us. Western psychology has drawn attention to the hidden depths of the mind, which can be accessed only in dreams and certain altered states, and through psychoanalysis or hypnosis. This implies that our minds are typically not only beyond our control but beyond our knowledge and understanding. Happily, the discipline of Zen can help us to rectify this. In fact, if we wish to make real progress in the Dharma (the search for the truth), it is essential to learn how to tame our mental waywardness.

Buddhist meditation teachers from all traditions instruct the practitioner to try and locate the point from which thoughts arise. As we try to do this in meditation, we come to recognize that thoughts arrive in the conscious mind suddenly, often taking us by surprise. Western psychology tells us they arise from the "unconscious" – a word used only to describe a process that we do not yet fully understand.

Even experienced meditators may never be able to reach the point where they see thoughts actually forming, but at least we can recognize the point at which they enter our consciousness, rather than becoming aware of them only when they are fully formed. A well-known Zen story illustrates this point. One day two monks were arguing about a flag blowing in the wind. One claimed it was the flag that was moving, the other argued that it was the wind. Overhearing them, the master said, "Neither the flag nor the wind is moving. It is your minds that are moving."

EXERCISE 14:
MONITOR YOUR THOUGHTS

As you watch your mind, you will notice that there are moments
of space in between thoughts when the mind is apparently free of
content. Yet something remains. What might this be? Do not pursue
such questions now, just notice them and keep watching your mind.

- Analyze what kind of thoughts your mind produces. What is their
  quality? Trivial? Profound? Optimistic? Anxious? Are there hopes
  and wishes, regrets and disappointments, fantasies and erotic
  daydreams? How does one thought set off another, leading to
  a train of associations? When thoughts arise, do not become
  lost in them or try to push them away, just monitor them.

- Probe deeper. What is the nature of thought itself? Is it just words?
  Do not pursue these questions during meditation, simply ask them.
  The answers will arise at some point of their own accord – if not
  today, then during some future meditation.

- Think over what you have learned about the nature of your own
  mind and try to bring something of this watchfulness into daily life.

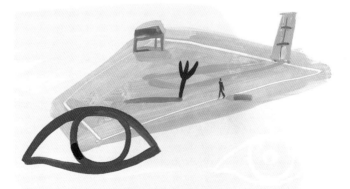

Movement and Stillness in the Mind

Zen teaches that everything we experience takes place within our minds, as shown in the story of the monks quarrelling about the movement of flags and the wind (see p.78). We only know the world "out there" when we have taken it inside our own minds (often misunderstanding and misinterpreting it in the process). In fact, our perception of the world is largely a process of creative imagination. The importance of recognizing this in order to reach an understanding of reality is emphasized by the Buddhist Yogachara philosophy, sometimes referred to as "mind-only", which influenced Soto Zen.

The minds of most of us are in constant movement. To recognize reality in the middle of all this movement is like a person trying to paint a landscape from the window of a fast-moving train. If through meditation our mind learns stillness, it can retain its own equanimity no matter how frantic the outside world. The Zen poet Shodoka expressed this succinctly in verse: "Walking is Zen. / Sitting too is Zen. / If I talk or say nothing, / if I rest or hurry along, / in essence everything is Unmoving."

"Unmoving" does not mean "without thoughts and emotions" – that would deprive us of our human nature. Rather, it denotes that the Zen mind is not pulled and pushed this way and that *by* thoughts and emotions. The "unmoving" mind enjoys thoughts and emotions, uses them creatively, is not disturbed by them, and can focus attention on them as it pleases. When we are beset by worries and anxieties, most of us are unable to lay them to rest. The "unmoving" mind has no such difficulties.

EXERCISE 15:
EXPLORE YOUR EMOTIONS

Zen teaches that when emotions arise during meditation you should not try to resist them, but instead explore them more deeply.

- Start with how you feel when you begin meditation. If you are experiencing reluctance, is it because you are bored? Or do you resent that you are not progressing fast enough? Observe these feelings. Recognize the thoughts with which they are associated, and notice the tricks your mind is playing in order to stop you gaining some control over it.

- As you meditate you may find a pleasant emotion arising. Or, you may feel that something is troubling you. Whatever the emotion examine it carefully. Is it a physical sensation? Is it causing tension in your body? Do not try too hard to answer these questions, simply observe your emotions, then let them go. The more you recognize them as bundles of physical sensations, the more you will realize that it is you who controls *them* rather than they who control *you*.

The Practice of Mindfulness

Zen teaches that part of our dissatisfaction with life arises from the fact that we have become so used to the world that we no longer notice its beauty and its infinite variety. But even the most mundane objects are things of wonder if we stop to look at them, and the fact that we are alive is the biggest wonder of all. So how do we learn fully to appreciate the world's beauty in our everyday life?

The answer can be summed up in one word: "attention". The concept of attention – or mindfulness, as it is called in Zen – was introduced in Chapter 1, and it is such a fundamental technique in Zen meditation that here we look at it more deeply.

The Buddha described the four foundations of mindfulness as: an awareness of our body's movements (mindfulness of the body); an awareness of our physical sensations (mindfulness of the feelings); an awareness of our moods and emotions (mindfulness of the mental state); and an awareness of our thoughts (mindfulness of mental objects). We can achieve mindfulness by focusing fully upon the present moment without being lost (as we usually are) in thoughts about the past or future, and in associated fantasies and anxieties. To be mentally absorbed in anything but the present is to be centred not in reality but in ideas *about* reality.

In *zazen* (sitting meditation), we are mindful of our breathing. This act reconciles the opposites of outer and

inner, the gross material of the body with the fine material of the breath, the conscious and unconscious minds (we can be conscious or unconscious of our breathing), and volitional and non-volitional activity (we can control our breathing or allow it to become automatic). In this way, mindfulness in *zazen* serves as an expression of the underlying unity of all life.

However, Zen teaches that mindfulness should be experienced not just in sitting meditation, but at all times.

In theory, few things should be easier; in practice, few things are more difficult. More often than not the mind refuses to stay in the present moment, preferring to pursue its own thoughts. But if we succeed in practising mindfulness in everyday life, we are rewarded by a number of priceless psychological benefits. Memory improves dramatically, for we are actually attending to what we are seeing and

doing. Our sensitivity to our environment deepens
as we become aware of the beauty around us that
previously went unnoticed. Colours, shapes – the
essential presence of the world, stand out with vividness.
And our affection for even the most ordinary objects grows as
the very sacredness of life becomes apparent in each moment.

There are equally valuable physical benefits. Mindfulness involves
being aware of our bodies as well as of the world around us. Through
focusing on our bodies we can become conscious of physical tensions
as they build up during the day, and take steps to release them as they
arise. Similarly, we can become conscious of the times
when one set of muscles seems to work against
another, instead of all our muscles moving in harmony. For example, notice what happens when you
stoop to pick up something after you have been
immobile for a while. Your body stiffens, resenting the
effort, and your movements are typically jerky, instead of fluid and
graceful as they should be. Zen urges us to learn from the natural, co-
ordinated way in which young children move, the lack of tension with
which they turn from one activity to another, as well as the absorption
they show when delighted by a particular object or pursuit.

*"If moment by moment
you can keep your mind
clear, then nothing will
confuse you ... "*
Sheng Yen

The same qualities are displayed by the Zen master. He or she
brings the same high level of attention to all tasks great and small –
whether tending a garden (see pp.44–7), painting a picture (see
pp.60–1) or preparing and serving tea (see pp.54–5). By introducing
mindfulness into our daily lives, we too can acquire something of the
ease of movement that the masters retain into old age, and the sense of
stillness and harmony that they exude.

EXERCISE 16: WATCH THE WORLD

Developing the ability to clear your mind of all clutter and to focus entirely on the present is fundamental to Zen practice. The following exercise helps us learn how to apply these skills to daily activities.

- Choose an everyday task, such as taking a shower, washing dishes, tidying your desk, gardening, or any other action that does not normally require you to give it your full attention.

- As you go about your task, maintain an internal commentary on what you are doing, using the word "now" as often as possible. For example, if you are washing the dishes, say to yourself: "I am now turning on the taps," "I am now hearing the sound of running water," and so on. Try to keep this up for at least 10 minutes.

- Analyze the effect that this mindfulness had upon how you saw the world. Did you experience a new-found wonder in your task (for example, perhaps you found the sound of running water melodic)? Try to recall each detail of the activity. What effect has the exercise had upon your memory of the event?

Mental Challenges in Meditation

One of my early meditation teachers once told me that if his students did not encounter some boredom during meditation, they were not actually meditating. What he meant is that the blissful state that some people experience during their practice is little more than self-indulgence. A Chinese Ch'an master described this state to me as "sitting in a cave with ghosts" – that is, a state of illusion rather than an experience of the reality of our own being.

Certainly meditation is a tranquil experience for much of the time – deeply relaxing both mentally and physically. And certainly it can be blissful.

But these states are not an end in themselves. If you experience them it may simply mean that you are in a light trance. And as with any emotions or feelings, bliss and tranquillity must be observed, not only to see into their nature, but to address the essential issue: "*Who* is actually tranquil or blissful?" Like all questions in Zen meditation, you should just hold it in your mind, rather than let your intellect work on it. Answers to such queries ulti-  mately arise by themselves, as an experience of intuitive knowledge rather than in the form of words.

Boredom can take many shapes and sizes. For some practitioners boredom is less a problem in the later stages of meditation than at the beginning. Once the novelty of the first few days wears off, meditation may seem flat and uninspiring, and the temptation to give up becomes strong. Again, as with other feelings, we need to explore this boredom. What is it? Is it a general physical restlessness? Or is it a realization that there are more pressing or more exciting activities that we could be doing? Notice this restlessness and the way in which the mind is attempting to entice you away with its promise of more interesting activities, and remind yourself that the reason you meditate is precisely to learn how to overcome such tendencies. And remember too that the clarity of mind and the improved ability to concentrate, which develop with regular meditation practice, will be useful in every area of your life.

Learning to quieten mental chatter is always a problem for the beginner, but our minds can cause chaos not only through thoughts in word form, but also through visionary experiences. Sometimes these visions are memories of places and people; at other times they seem to be original creations of our own mind. In fact, the only limitations are the limitations of our imagination. Such visions are normally pleasant experiences and can be so enticing that there is a temptation just to sit there and enjoy them. For example, you might envisage an exotic location, such as a tropical island with beautiful white beaches, lapped by turquoise seas; or you might see dreamy landscapes with mythical beasts or legendary heroes. Sometimes the visions can be weird or gothic, depicting strange cities with narrow, winding streets or beautiful women in fairytale castles. Occasionally, your mind might conjure up distressing scenes of war and strife featuring armed men, hideous faces or starving children, which may be so disturbing that they force you to cut short your meditation session. How, then, can you learn to banish such strangely captivating distractions?

Once again, the crucial thing is to try to avoid becoming caught up in these visions or identifying with them. Remember that they are all simply creations of your own mind, and are no more substantial than your dreams. Once you begin to practise meditation with your eyes open, rather than closed, such visual distractions usually cease, but in any case, by refusing to be diverted by them you are strengthening the power of your mind. This mental strength can help you to cease being at the mercy of wandering concentration in daily life, especially when you are carrying out vital tasks. Be aware also that when distracting thoughts arise, they are often accompanied by a tensing of the muscles, as your body gears up to head off elsewhere. Make a mental note of this tension, then try to relax and let it go.

EXERCISE 17:
PRACTISE WALKING MEDITATION

Zen monks perform walking meditation, or *kinhin*, in the intervals between sitting meditation. In Rinzai Zen, *kinhin* is practised briskly, but in Soto Zen it is undertaken slowly, with dignity, as recommended in this exercise. Aim to perform *kinhin* for at least 5 minutes at a time.

- Adopt the correct posture. Place your right fist, with thumb inside, just above your navel, cover it with the left palm, and keep your elbows at right angles to your body. Try to choose somewhere that allows you to walk forward at least 10 feet (3 m) before turning and retracing your steps.

- Synchronize your steps with your breath, stepping forward only 6 inches (40 cm) each time. Raise your rear foot as you inhale, bring it past your stationary foot as the in-breath is completed, place it down and move forward as you exhale. Walk so that your foot seems to sink into the ground, heel first. Keeping your steps and breath synchronized, allow your attention to focus upon your movement, your shifting from one foot to the other, and the sensation of the ground beneath your feet.

Zen and the Golden Flower

The early influence of Daoism contributed not only to Zen's emphasis upon the natural world but also to an interest in the subtle energy systems within the human body. Union between the spiritual and physical principles was seen as a way of gaining influence over the autonomic nervous system (as witnessed in the "superhuman" feats of martial arts practitioners), as well as being important to the realization of reality. Control of the breath, the life force linking spirit and body, was regarded as essential if physical and spiritual union was to be effected. Zen rejected the Daoist belief that breath control could lead to physical immortality, but nevertheless considered that it contributed to our ability to remain fully conscious and in command of our destiny, even as we die.

In Daoism, the "golden flower" was used as a symbol for the life force (*qi* in Chinese and *ki* in Japanese). Practitioners were taught, through breath control, to circulate this life force around the body and then to "fix" it in the "centre of emptiness" at the crown of the head, thus empowering the true seat of consciousness. Such complex breathing techniques should only be practised with an expert teacher, but the exercise opposite is an introductory practice, often taught in Zen, which allows us to control the breath and to experience both physical and psychological benefits as a result. This technique is also a powerful aid to concentration, so you may wish to use it during meditation instead of focusing upon the sensations of air entering and exiting your nostrils (see p.69).

90

EXERCISE 18:
SENSE YOUR INNER ENERGY

This exercise teaches you to become aware of your inner energy through the Zen technique of "circular breathing", which is based on a practice sometimes known as "Daoist yoga".

● Sit in your usual meditation position and breathe steadily in and out through your nose. Imagine that you are drawing air in through the base *chakra* (one of seven energy centres in the body according to

yoga), located at the perineum. As you draw breath in, imagine that it flows upward until it reaches your heart area. Then as you breathe out, visualize the air flowing down outside your body to join the air of the next in-breath.

● You will soon become aware that you are breathing deeply, as your breath starts as low down as possible, and then fills your lungs to the top of your chest. Do you also notice a feeling of coolness at the base *chakra* as you breathe in? And then a sensation of warmth in front of the base *chakra*, as the out-breath flows back into your body? Do not worry whether this is real or imaginary – simply be aware of the sensation, and the feeling of inner energy flowing upward, as it completes the circle on the out-breath to return into the body.

The Art of T'ai Chi

We tend to think of meditation primarily as a seated practice, but there are a number of moving meditations that combine mind training with physical exercise, leading to control not only of mental processes but also of the energy flows within the body. Perhaps the best-known is t'ai chi, which is associated more closely with Daoism than with Zen, but many Zen practitioners are also t'ai chi adepts, and the two traditions complement each other in a number of ways.

The origins of t'ai chi date back to the fourteenth century, when the Daoist priest Chang-san Feng had a dream in which a god taught him a new series of movements. Shortly afterward he observed a crane fighting a snake, and noticed how each animal used submission and pliability to avoid the other, and to launch its own attack, thus confirming the principles behind the movements shown in his dream.

T'ai chi sequences (known as "forms") are practised slowly, deliberately and with total mindfulness. It is claimed that they follow nature's own pathways of energy, thus putting body and mind in harmony with natural forces. During the movements your body remains in perfect balance, with the focus of attention placed in the *tan t'ien* (the point two finger-breadths below the navel where energy is said to accumulate). In the basic posture your spine should be "erect as a stack of coins", your head held poised as if suspended by a "thread from the heavens", and your lower body fully grounded. It is best to study t'ai chi with a properly qualified teacher, because much learning takes place (as with Zen art, and haiku writing) from watching and copying a master.

EXERCISE 19: SCOOP THE STREAM

Practitioners of t'ai chi usually also perform Qigong exercises, which
work on the same principles of inner energy, but are primarily static.
They also closely resemble many of the exercises done by Zen monks
to restore suppleness after each meditation session. The following
Qigong exercise, which is known as "Scooping the Stream", is one
of the simplest and most pleasant to enact.

- Stand, feet together, hands loosely by your sides, eyes fixed on a
  chosen point ahead. Inhale slowly as you raise your arms above
  your head to interlace your fingers, the palms of your hands facing
  upward. Keeping your heels on the ground, stretch your body
  upward to its full extent and count to 3. Exhale slowly as you
  lower your arms to your sides. Pause and count to 3 again.

- Bring your hands in front of your navel, turn your palms upward,
  and interlace your fingers to form a "scoop". Slowly inhale while
  raising your arms to bring the scoop to your lips as if you are
  drinking water, with your elbows as high as you can. Hold this
  position for a count of three. Turn your palms downward and lower
  your arms again, exhaling slowly. Repeat the whole sequence 6 times.

The Way of the Peaceful Warrior

Legend has it that sixth-century Zen monks, prevented from carrying weapons by their vows of non-violence, found themselves easy prey to attack outside the monastery. In response they developed a highly successful martial art, a form of self-defence (*wu shu*) that relied only on empty hands. This approach depended upon three things. First, the monks' meditation training allowed them to remain calm during combat and to focus their attention exclusively upon an opponent. Second, this training enabled them to direct their inner life energy to various parts of the body, rendering them immune from harm. And third, their desire to avoid directly causing suffering led them to use their opponent's strength against himself.

" The art of [Zen] archery means a profound and far-reaching contest of the archer with himself ... . You will see with other eyes and measure with other measures ... it happens to all who are touched by the spirit of this art."

Kenzo Awa

The monks realized that *wu shu* was a true test of the meditator's progress in that success or failure depended upon his power to focus the mind. Over the centuries other martial arts developed, some employing weapons, but the spiritual emphasis remained.

In teaching Zen archery Master Kenzo Awa advised pupils to stand "egoless at the point of highest tension" – to remain focused each time they drew the powerful bow. Only thus would the arrow be loosed without the slightest sign of tension toward the target. As in archery, so in life: the Zen practitioner remains egoless – freed from the dictates of the artificial self that craves such things as gratification, escape and prestige – even when faced with life's greatest challenges.

EXERCISE 20: RIDE A ZEN HORSE

Zen places great emphasis on the mind–body interaction. The more focused and disciplined the mind, the better it controls the body and resists its distractions; the better trained the body, the more it serves the mind. The martial arts are a training *par excellence* for both mind and body. Proficiency demands long practice with a qualified teacher, but this simple exercise (the "horse-riding stance"), used in all the martial arts and said to accumulate *ki*, is a good introduction, and graphically illustrates what is meant by being "egoless at the point of highest tension".

- Stand with your feet shoulder-width apart. Bring your fists into your sides, palms uppermost. Now bend at the knees, keeping your back straight and lower yourself into a sitting posture. Hold the position, breathing evenly and deeply.

- After a short interval the posture becomes slightly uncomfortable. Note how the ego (the "self") immediately wants to be released from discomfort. Try to observe this demand without identifying with it, and keep your mind relaxed. (Likewise, resist if your ego has an alternative strategy, such as to urge you to hang on with grim determination until you find the position untenable.) Let your body gauge when you should end the exercise.

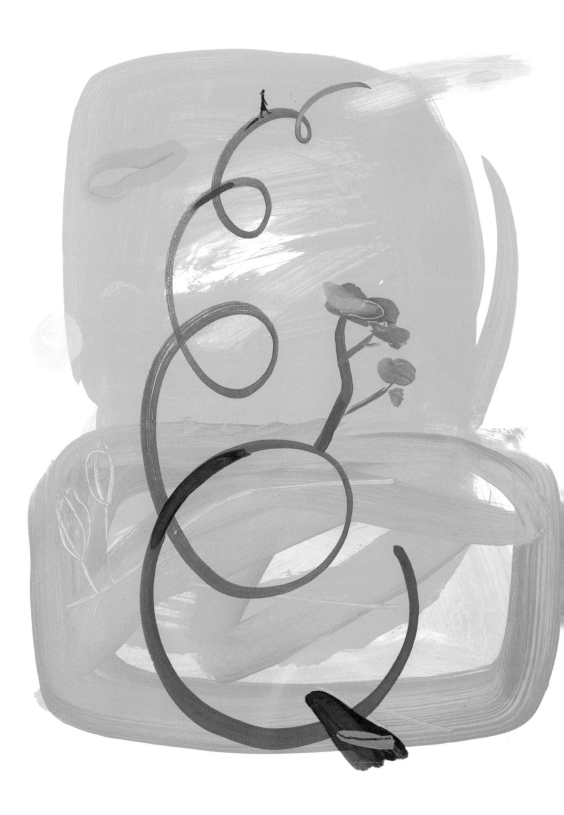

CHAPTER 4

WALKING ON

Zen practice is a journey. Sometimes we find the path deceptively easy and at other times deceptively hard; sometimes we lose our way, and sometimes we backtrack. Try not to feel that by this point in the book you should have achieved a particular level of competence. Remember that Zen is "your ordinary, everyday life" lived reflectively: there are no schedules or timescales, and the way forward is simply to look around you, see where you are, and move on.

Wherever we are, we have already made good headway on our journey. The very process of taking an interest in Zen, practising meditation on a regular basis, and practising mindfulness in all our activities take us far along the path. In this chapter we develop our practice further by deepening our awareness using techniques such as direct contemplation and wall-gazing. We explore life in a Zen monastery, discover Zen retreats and learn about one of the most fascinating aids to practice – the koan.

Deepening Awareness

Zen meditation is fundamentally about awareness – an awareness that begins with sitting on a cushion and observing the breath as consciousness spreads outward until it pervades each moment of waking life. You are aware of yourself, of the outer world, and of the relationship between the two. As your practice develops, so your awareness deepens. The first step toward enhancing this awareness is to pay more attention to the state of mind in which you sit.

Dogen, the founder of the Soto Zen tradition, insisted that we must sit with a sense of gratitude – gratitude for the gift of a precious human life, for the breath that sustains life, for the traditions that have handed the practice of meditation down to us, and for the awe-inspiring phenomena of the natural world and the source from which they arise. By entering meditation with gratitude in mind, the sense of thankfulness begins to flow not only through the sitting meditation session itself, but into all aspects of life, and we begin to recognize how wonderful it is actually to be alive.

But this state of mind – thankful, open, accepting, loving – is often short-lived as it becomes overshadowed all too frequently by distracting mental chatter. Instead of deepening, our awareness becomes caught up once more in superficial, discursive, unproductive thinking. At this point, Zen introduces a deceptively simple but remarkably effective strategy. Rather as in the exercise on p.85, the meditator comments upon the thing of which he or she is aware, in this case thinking. But in contrast to that exercise, the commentary is kept to a minimum. The meditator merely repeats silently "thinking, thinking, thinking". This has the dual effect of distancing your mind from its content, and of revealing the often trivial nature of your thoughts. For example, in the case of gratitude, you realize that it is not a superficial form of self-congratulation, but rather a word rich with positive significance – gratitude is a state of being and a reaching-out with warmth.

"If you are unable to find the truth right where you are, where else do you expect to find it?"

Dogen

By distancing your mind from its contents, a further, deeper revelation sometimes emerges, namely that it is not thinking itself that is at fault, but what we *do* with our thinking. Contrary to popular belief, Zen is not anti-thinking nor anti-intellectual. Its prime concern is that we do not let our intellect take us away from the direct experience of reality, and from gratitude and sensitivity toward the world in which we live.

Beyond the Opposites

We have seen that the form of a cup and the emptiness enclosed within it (see p.55) are both essential to its nature. These apparent opposites are therefore simply aspects of the unity that we know as a cup. The same is true of pairs of opposites in general: light and dark, old and young, male and female, and so on. Each of these is defined by its opposite – without its opposite it could not be said to exist. So each member of a pair is an aspect of the other member, and is therefore also an aspect of the unity that encompasses them both.

However, in much of our Western thinking, we separate things. Our love of categorizing means that we isolate them, conveying the impression that existence is made up of individual objects and people. Our methods of philosophical enquiry add to the appearance of individuality – something is *either* this *or* that. In contrast, Zen accepts the concept that something can be *both* this *and* that simultaneously. For example, the days of the week are both real and unreal: they are real to us and we plan our lives by them; but they are unreal to nature, which makes no distinction between, say, a Sunday and a Monday.

"When the opposites arise, the Buddha mind is lost."
Zen saying

Putting things into categories can also lead to conflict: you *either* agree with me *or* disagree. If you agree, you are on my side; if you disagree, you are not. This is not the way of Zen.

In meditation it becomes apparent that something can be both *this* and *that*: the parts of our body, our in-breath and out-breath, our mind and the outside world, are all unified aspects of self and all existence.

We cannot force this sense of unity – it will arise when the moment is right. But we can increase our awareness of it by using our body as a focus at the start of each meditation session. First, concentrate in turn upon each of your paired body-parts – your limbs, ears, eyes, and so on. Ask yourself how each pair feels. Then consider how each half can act and sense things independently of its partner, or act together with it. Reflect on the apparent paradox that the members of each pair are opposites, yet they are also elements of a larger whole – your body – which is, in turn, part of you as an entity. Finally, consider your own place in the universal oneness of which we are all a part, from which we all arise, and to which we all return.

Form is Emptiness, Emptiness is Form

As our awareness deepens, so the relationship between form and emptiness becomes clearer. The world is seen as a constant interplay between the two, and the *Heart Sutra*, which is chanted everyday in Zen monastries, tells us that form *is* in fact emptiness, and emptiness *is* form. Zen invites us to examine this interplay and the very nature of form and emptiness.

The closer we look, the more we realize that not only do form and emptiness define each other (where one begins, the other ends), but that form itself is "empty" of any permanent self-nature. Even the most enduring forms, such as rocks and mountains, eventually crumble into other forms. And where is the enduring form in an object such as a table? If we dismantle the table into four legs and a top, where now is the table?. If we cut up the legs and the top, where is *their* self-nature? Similarly, the space around us has "form" in that it is bounded by objects, but if these objects are removed or rearranged, the space changes into a quite different "form". It is the same with the mind. While a thought is present in the mind, the mind experiences "form", but as each thought passes away the mind experiences emptiness.

However, if descriptions such as these could give us a complete explanation of form and emptiness, there would be no need to meditate upon them. We must regard them therefore as simply a place at which to start our enquiry and use meditation to help us grasp their true nature.

EXERCISE 21: CONTEMPLATE AN OBJECT

Direct contemplation of an object is an opportunity to learn what Master Yunyen called "the teachings given by inanimate things". This can lead to an insight into the relationship between the apparent (relative reality) and the absolute – the underlying emptiness and infinite potential from which the world of form arises (ultimate reality). But do not try to force this (or any other) realization – it will appear when your mind develops the right level of attention.

- Select an object that is apparently commonplace, such as a small plant, and focus upon it for the whole of your meditation session.

- Define the characteristics of your chosen object in your mind. Consider its uniqueness and its place in a universal context. Try to see it simply as it *is*, without judgment. Learn how even such a mundane object can be a thing of wonder, if you really *look* at it.

- Use a different object each time you meditate in this way. You can also practise outside formal meditation, at any time when you are able to relax your mind and focus entirely on a single item.

Bodhidharma and His Cave

The story goes that when Bodhidharma, the first Zen patriarch, brought his form of Buddhism from India to China in the sixth century CE, he was invited for an audience with Emperor Wu of the Liang Dynasty, who was famous for his philanthropy. When the emperor asked Bodhidharma how much merit had accrued from all the good works that he had performed during his reign, the patriarch replied that merit leading to salvation could not be accumulated in this way. Taken aback at the apparent audacity of this answer, the emperor then asked who it was who stood before him, and Bodhidharma replied that he had no idea.

Not surprisingly the interview ended abruptly. But the tale shows that the emperor had failed to understand the Zen doctrine of emptiness – that neither he (through his good deeds) nor Bodhidharma had achieved ultimate existence. If the emperor had been attentive at the end of the interview, he might have experienced the moment of sudden enlightenment – seeing into the true nature of things – that sometimes arises in response to cryptic responses by Zen masters.

After leaving Emperor Wu, we are told that Bodhidharma retired to a cave and meditated facing a wall for nine years. To overcome tiredness he cut off his eyelids, and the first tea plants sprang from his drops of blood. Zen does not waste time arguing over the truth or otherwise of this story. Instead, it leaves the tale to serve not only as a perfect example of dedication to practice, but also of a method of practice itself (wall-gazing), and of the good things (the tea plants) that can arise out of suffering.

EXERCISE 22: FACE THE WALL

Few of us would be capable of emulating Bodhidharma's nine years of wall-gazing in a cave, and even fewer of us would want to try! But Soto Zen makes particular use of the practice for regular meditation sessions, and it can be a useful aid to concentration.

- Position your cushion so that you are 12–18 inches (about 30–45 cm) from a blank wall, and sit as usual in meditation. (Try not to use a wall that has distracting wallpaper, and avoid any with pictures or other decorations.)

- Concentrate on your breathing until you settle. Then, through half-closed eyelids, look steadily at the wall. Avoid blinking for as long as you can, but when you must blink, do so slowly and deliberately.

- Try not to be distracted by any patterns you see in the surface of the wall, or by "projected" images from your imagination. Simply return each time to the solidity of the wall. (If this proves difficult, remind yourself that if Bodhidharma could do it for nine years, the rest of us should be able to manage at least half an hour!)

Zen Monasteries and Monks

In a Zen monastery, the first thing likely to strike you is the tranquillity, followed by the sense of order and, if no ceremony is in progress, the silence. Monks may be meditating in the Zen hall, or going mindfully about their duties. There is an indefinable sense of presence.

Originally, Zen was not a monastic tradition. Pupils studied with individual masters, with the emphasis upon direct transmission of the teachings from master to pupil. But then, as advanced masters attracted large groups of followers, rules and regulations became necessary for all these people to live and study together harmoniously.

THE ZEN PRECEPTS

All Zen monks vow to follow the four lay precepts, made up of the first two of the Ten Great Precepts (see right), in addition to the prohibition of alcohol and illicit sex. They observe a wide range of rules, but of particular importance are:

The Three Pure Precepts

1. Refrain from evil
2. Do only good [in your inner life – thoughts, meditation]
3. Do good for others [in your outer life – show compassion, avoid violence, and so on]

The Ten Great Precepts

1. Do not kill
2. Do not steal
3. Do not covet
4. Do not tell untruths
5. Do not spread delusion
6. Do not speak ill of other people
7. Do not be proud or devalue other people
8. Do not be ungenerous
9. Do not be angry
10. Do not defame the three treasures – Buddha, Dharma and Sangha

Establishing a community in this way also benefited individuals by providing them with support and guidance from other students as well as their masters.

Many of the monasteries' rules were first laid down by Dogen, the founder of Soto Zen. Junior monks had to show respect to senior monks in ways that might seem bizarre to the Westerner. For example, a junior monk was not allowed to touch the senior nor any part of his own head or body in the senior's presence. There were 62 rules in total! The principle of respect is still observed – respect is shown to the individual because the teachings that he or she receives in the monastery demand respect. You might like to demonstrate your own respect for Zen meditation by introducing a ritual, such as bowing to your cushion (see pp.74–7).

"A monk asked Chao-chou, 'If a poor man comes, what should one give him?' 'Nothing, as he lacks nothing,' answered the master."
Zen mondo

The Zen Retreat

In addition to daily meditation, from time to time Zen teachers conduct *sesshin*s (retreats) for students, consisting of seven-day (or longer) periods of intensive practice taken in silence (except during private interviews with the Zen master). Typically, the *sesshin* starts at 4.30 am with the first period of sitting and ends at 9 or 10 pm. In between, there are some fifteen half-hour periods of sitting meditation interspersed with walking meditation, ceremonies, meals, interviews, work periods, teaching and one or more brief rest periods (during which students are encouraged to pursue individual meditation).

In Soto Zen, practitioners undertake wall-gazing meditation (see p.105), while in Rinzai Zen they face into the Zen Hall and typically work on koans. A senior monk or practitioner patrols the Hall carrying the *keisaku*, the flat stick used to whack the shoulder of anyone who signifies, with a bow, the need for attention.

The Zen *sesshin* is demanding on both body and mind, and is suitable only for advanced practitioners. Ch'an master Sheng Yen lists its purpose thus: to enable the practitioner to recognize the extent to which the mind is out of control; to learn how to train the mind; to experience the calm mind; to take opportunities for repentance and purification; and to practise meditation in the way most likely to lead the individual to enlightenment. In addition, the *sesshin* allows the practitioner to experience a strict regime and thus to recognize the nature of the ego, with its craving for self-assertion and creature comforts. The *sesshin* can also help the Westerner realize the superficial nature of many things deemed indispensable in the outside world.

EMPTINESS IN THE HAND

Because of the intensity and sheer amount of time spent in meditation during a *sesshin*, it is not uncommon for practitioners to experience sudden moments of enlightenment – extraordinary insights in which certain things about the nature of reality become clear. Everyone experiences realization in their own way, but we can gain much by contemplating fellow practitioners' accounts of enlightenment. Take, for example, the experience of the elderly Japanese Zen nun Chiyono.

After many years of study without enlightenment, Chiyono was walking across the yard one night, carrying an old bamboo pail full of water in which she could see a reflection of the moon. Suddenly, the handle broke, the water spilled, the moon's reflection disappeared, and Chiyono was enlightened. She explained her experience in this poem: "This way and that way / I tried to keep the pail together / Hoping the weak bamboo / Would never break. / Suddenly the bottom fell out / No more water / No more moon in the water / Emptiness in my hand!"

It is worth spending some time reflecting on this poem, rather as if you are tasting something sweet. Ask yourself what the verse communicates to you about Chiyono and her Zen practice. How is this applicable to you, your practice and your own mind?

Zen and the Art of Paradox

Zen is constantly pulling us up short, stopping us in our tracks, prompting us to look afresh at life and ourselves, and thus helping us to break free from illusory ways of thinking. The Zen mind is not fooled by the artificial meanings and explanations that conventional wisdom imposes upon life. Like a compassionate but rather irritating friend, the Zen mind demands that we say what we see, not what we think we see. It insists that we recognize for ourselves that intellect, for all its value in certain practical ways, has its limitations. The intellect works by dichotomizing the world, breaking it into opposites, defining everything in terms of what it is not, fragmenting reality into a myriad isolated, individual things. By contrast, Zen sees the essential interconnectedness, the interdependence, ultimately the unity of all phenomena, including our thoughts and experiences, each of which arises from our previous thoughts and experiences, our previous interactions with both inner and outer worlds, our personal and our cultural histories, in fact the experiences of all humankind back to beginningless time.

The undeniable accuracy of this way of looking at the world brings us face to face with a teasing paradox. As we already know (see p.100), things are both separate from each other, and not separate from each other. Separateness presents us with the relative reality, non-separateness with the ultimate reality of existence. It is one thing to recognize this fact, but it is quite another directly to know it – an experience sometimes referred to as a "turning about in the deepest state of consciousness", which changes

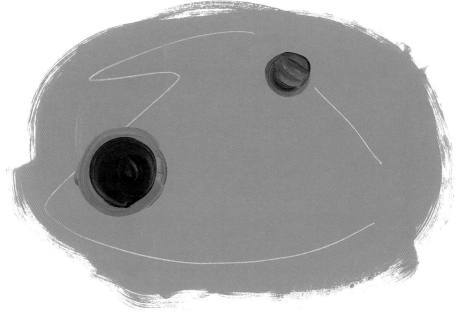

our view of the world and of ourselves not by intellectual debate but by a profound re-orientation of our whole being. All Zen training points us toward this experience, but Rinzai Zen in addition emphasizes the koan, which at first glance appears to be a bizarre, seemingly ridiculous question or statement. It does not take long for us to realize that the koan cannot be understood by rational thought.

Some koans consist simply of enigmatic statements, while others are strange dialogues of questions and answers between monks and their teachers. There are two main collections of koans: *The Gateless Gate* (known in Japanese as *Mumonkan*) and *The Blue Cliff Record* (in Japanese, *Hekiganroku*). Both contain koans devised by centuries of Zen masters, together with commentaries added by other Zen masters, which at first sight are even more paradoxical and enigmatic than the koans themselves. The Japanese Zen master Hakuin (see p.115) was so convinced of the value of koans that he dismissed both the wall-gazing used in Soto Zen (see pp.104–5) and the mantra meditation used in Pure Land Buddhism (see pp.128–9) and focused his practice on koans.

How then are koans used in meditation? The Zen practitioner works on a koan while he or she meditates, keeping the question or statement in the forefront of awareness, until he or she feels that a resolution has been reached. The answer is then taken to the master, who listens and, like as not, shakes his or her head and sends the practitioner back to their meditation cushion.

In the exercise opposite we take the koan known as "Joshu's Mu", which is frequently given to beginners, and learn various ways to approach and unravel it. But before you do the exercise, it is worth bearing in mind the following conversation between a Zen master and one of his pupils. The pupil asked "What is the Great Way?" to which the master replied, "It is right before you." "Then why don't I see it?" returned the pupil. "Because", answered the master, "you are thinking of yourself."

Another of the best-known koans, and one that perfectly illustrates the paradoxical nature of these bizarre questions, is "What is the sound of one hand clapping?" By definition, clapping involves two hands. So how can one hand clap? There is no logical answer. And yet there *is* an answer, or rather a resolution.

However, the resolution is not simply a form of words, and so it would be useless to offer examples here. Two practitioners may give exactly the same answer, and the master may accept it from one yet reject it from the other. Resolving a koan is not just about *what* is said, but *how* it is said, which tells the master whether the person is using

EXERCISE 23: DISCOVER THE KOAN

The first koan often given to practitioners is known as "Joshu's Mu". When the eighth-century master Joshu was asked "Has a dog Buddha-nature?", he replied "Mu", which translates literally as "No". In the following exercise we explore ways in which to meditate on this koan.

- Start your meditation, keeping the koan in your mind. Ponder why, if all beings have a Buddha-nature, Joshu said that a dog has none.

- Be aware that the moment distracting thoughts arise, it is your "dog" mind trying to take over. Respond by bringing "mu" or "no" (it is often easier for Westerners to use the English word) into the forefront of awareness.

- Remember that "no" is not negative in this context, it is an affirmation that there *is* a Buddha-nature, that there *is* ultimate reality, but that these are not revealed by discursive thinking, compulsive rationalization or conventional perception.

- Try to use the same method outside formal meditation to help you recognize and say "no" to desultory thoughts each time they arise.

his or her intellect or has really glimpsed the nature of reality. Some years ago a book was published purporting to give the "answers" to all the best-known koans, but such a book is of no real help. If you went to the master having memorized one of these "answers", he or she would see through the pretence straight away, and send you away with hardly a glance.

Koan meditation, which is often used as an alternative in Zen to *zazen* (sitting meditation), is not intended to give the busy mind a question or statement to think about. Rather, it is designed to free our minds from the illusion that our normal state of automatic thinking represents real consciousness. Whatever you think or imagine is a product of your mind, it is not the essence of your mind. And without direct experience of the essence of your mind, it is impossible to evaluate the reality of anything conceived in or perceived by consciousness.

> *"One day a monk made a request to Joshu: 'I have just entered the monastery. Please give me instruction.' Joshu asked, 'Have you had your breakfast?' 'Yes, I have,' replied the monk. 'Then wash your bowls,' said Joshu. The monk had a realization."*
>
> Zen koan

The koan is a concentration device that constantly prompts the mind to stop indulging in the random thinking of ordinary consciousness. Once this mental chatter is stopped, the Zen practitioner's artificial world view, which is conditioned and composed by such thinking, is also halted. In other words, his or her personal idea of reality, which is built upon the limitations of fixed ideas and habits of thought, is suspended, thus opening his or her mind to true reality.

MASTER HAKUIN'S GRADES

The Japanese Zen master Hakuin (1686–1789) was so emphatic about the value of koan meditation that he standardized koans within Rinzai Zen, classifying them into five progressively harder levels. Pupils were encouraged to proceed to the next grade only when the master had accepted their resolution of the koans at the preceding grade. The five levels (in ascending order of difficulty) are:

1. **Hosshin koans**, which give insight into emptiness, the essential essence of all things, the undifferentiated realm. A good example is: "With hands of emptiness I take hold of the plough; while walking I ride the water buffalo."

2. **Kikan koans**, which lead to a better understanding of the differentiated (phenomenal) world as seen through the eye of enlightenment. An example is the question "What is the meaning of Bodhidharma coming from the West?" followed by the answer "The cypress tree in the garden."

3. **Gonsen koans**, which help clarify the difficult words of Zen masters and open up a hidden world of beauty and wisdom. One such koan is the question "Speech and silence are concerned with subject and object. How can I transcend both subject and object?" followed by the answer "I always think of Konan [a province in China] in March. Partridges chirp among the fragrant blossoms."

4. **Nanto koans**, which point to a subtle place beyond all opposites and lead to tranquillity amid life's vicissitudes. For example: "It is like a water buffalo passing through a window; its head, horns and four legs all pass through, why can't its tail pass?"

5. **Goi koans**, the most difficult of all, which are associated with verses composed by Master Tozan Ryokai, and lead to final insight into the apparent and the real. A typical example is: "In such a wide world, why put on ceremonial robes and answer the bell?"

CHAPTER 5

COMPLETING THE CIRCLE

Zen is immediate and practical, but it is also transcendent and transpersonal, reminding us always that there is an ultimate reality beyond appearances. In Western culture there is a tendency to reinterpret Zen purely in terms of human psychology, and to write off any reference to other dimensions as of only symbolic value. This is not only to miss the essence of the teachings, but also to ignore the spiritual hunger that helps to make us human.

In this chapter, as we come full circle on our journey, we confront some of the more complex and spiritual aspects of Zen. We explore the master–pupil relationship and the ways in which we can learn from the Zen masters, through interviews and from studying their teachings. We examine the concept of Bodhisattvas (altruistic beings who refrain from entering Nirvana in order to help all other sentient beings); we consider Zen's affinities with Pure Land Buddhism; and we come face-to-face with the fundamental question and ultimate koan: "What (or who) am I?"

Master and Pupil

Owing to its enigmatic nature, Zen can be easily misunderstood or remain inscrutable. This perhaps explains why the Zen tradition has always placed great emphasis upon the master–pupil relationship. Practising under the guidance of a master creates a special relationship in that, by agreeing to take responsibility for the pupil, the master also takes responsibility for the student's failings. In return for this potentially heavy burden, the master expects great respect and total obedience from the pupil. However, there is no coercion in Zen. If you are unable to make progress with a particular master, you are free to leave

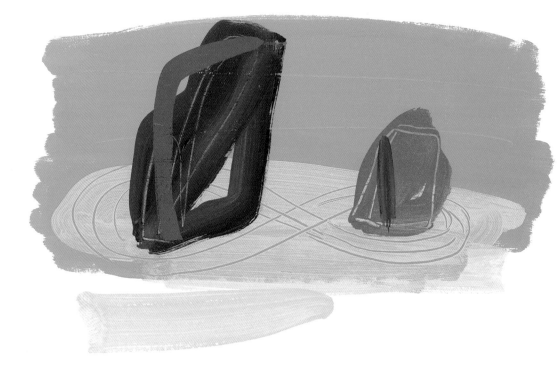

with the master's blessing. But if you choose to stay, then you must follow all his or her instructions to the letter.

The Zen master's manner is often as enigmatic as the koan. Curtness, even rudeness, is sometimes employed, but only to make the pupil confront his or her own ego. For example, a scholar, who had spent many years puzzling how the trees and grass could become enlightened, asked Zen master Shinkan if such a teaching were true. Shinkan answered, "Of what use is it to discuss how grass and trees become enlightened? The question is how do you yourself become enlightened. Did you ever consider that?" By his seeming rudeness, Shinkan enabled the scholar to see that academic questions are a waste of time – Zen teaches that we must always start with our own mind.

MASTER BANKEI'S WISDOM

There is no doubt that working with a Zen master can be very valuable, especially when we are experiencing difficulties with our practice. However, we would be disappointed if we expected him or her to lavish us with praise, even when we have made significant progress.

In fact, in the Zen tradition, praise (when it is given at all) often turns out to be another form of criticism. Take, for example, the story of seventeenth-century Master Bankei. He was petitioned by his pupils to send away one of their number who had been caught stealing. The students were outraged and insisted that if the thief did not leave, they would.

Bankei called all his pupils together and complimented them on their high moral values. However, he then added, "But our poor brother does not yet know right from wrong. Who will teach him if I do not? You all may leave if you wish; he stays." Of course, Bankei's stance encouraged the pupils to reconsider their attitude, and harmony was once again restored.

The Zen Interview

The formal interview (*dokusan*) between master and pupil is an important part of Zen meditation training. The pupil goes to the master's room, rings a bell to indicate his or her presence, enters when called, prostrates him- or herself, and asks questions or explains difficulties with practice. For example, beginners are likely to have concerns over topics such as postures and concentration, while more advanced practitioners may wish to discuss teachings or koans. The master always listens, sometimes answers, and sometimes simply rings his or her own bell indicating that the interview is at an end. The pupil prostrates him- or herself again and withdraws. Even the master's silence is regarded as an answer to the pupil's problem.

"Wordiness and intellection; the more we cling to them, the further astray we go."
Huineng

Such interviews are helpful to both the master (to monitor the pupil's progress) and the pupil (to gain expert help in resolving problems with practice).

Often the pupil uses the private interview to offer the resolution to a koan upon which he or she has been meditating. For example, take the meeting between Mamiya, who was already an accomplished practitioner, and his master. The koan on which Mamiya had been working is the well-known, "What is the sound of one hand clapping?" (see p.112), and Mamiya was unable to make any progress. "You are not working hard enough," his teacher told him, "You are too attached to food, to wealth, and to that sound [of one hand clapping]. It would be better if you died. That would solve the problem." Much abashed, Mamiya withdrew and meditated further on the koan. At the

next *dokusan* his teacher asked him what he had to show on the subject of the koan. Mamiya responded by falling down as if he were dead. "You are dead all right," responded the master, "now what about the sound of one hand clapping?" "I haven't solved it yet," answered the disappointed Mamiya. "Dead men do not speak," snapped his teacher, "Get out!" By falling down as if dead Mamiya demonstrated that the response to a koan can be an action rather than words. As we have seen, unfortunately he was unable to follow up his promising start. Try considering what you think went wrong for Mamiya as part of your own meditation practice.

When a pupil comes to the master with the resolution to a koan, the master may cut through any procrastination by shouting "Speak now!" or by seizing and shaking the pupil, or even by striking him. This is an attempt to encourage the student to recognize the immediacy of the present moment. The resolution to the koan is here, now, at this particular moment – there is no need to look anywhere else, either inside or outside the mind.

The master is also looking for spontaneity. If the resolution has come to the pupil, he or she will be bursting to communicate it. There will be no hesitation, no reflection, no cleverness with words. The "great ball of doubt", which Zen tells us the koan must become inside us, will have exploded into a new way of seeing and of being.

The Zen master is no fool. Remember that he or she has experienced the same problems, battled against the same frustrations and enerally trodden the same path as the pupil, so he or she can recognize instantly whether the student has had a true insight or not. For this reason, it is said that a pupil's realization must always be presented to and acknowledged by a master before it can be regarded as authentic.

EXERCISE 24:
CONSIDER "NANSEN'S GOOSE"

The Zen master can tell instantly whether or not a pupil has truly solved a koan. This exercise is designed to help you begin to recognize the difference between a manufactured and a spontaneous resolution. (But remember, you are learning how to work with koans – you are not trying to become a Zen master or obtain instant enlightement.)

● Consider the koan "Nansen's Goose". One day, a court official named Riko approached Zen master Nansen and asked him "If a man puts a gosling in a bottle, feeds it everyday until it grows into a goose and there is no more room in the bottle, how can he get the goose out without killing it or breaking the bottle?" "Riko!" shouted Nansen, and gave a loud clap with his hands. "Yes master?" asked the startled Riko. "See," said Nansen, "the goose is out!"

● Try to solve the koan logically. How could one get the goose out of the bottle without killing it or breaking the glass? And what relevance was Nansen's shout of "Riko" and his clap? Do not look for a catch; treat the koan as a riddle. Spend as long as you wish "manufacturing" answers and note them down.

● Hold the koan in your mind while meditating. Do not try to "solve" it. Imagine you are addressing it to a wise friend who sits opposite, listens, but does not answer. Now see what arises spontaneously in your mind.

● Compare the results from the two approaches, noting the different ways in which your mind responded to the koan. Which approach brought you most insight and why?

Experiences of the Zen Masters

A great deal can be learned about Zen meditation by studying the lives of Zen masters. Bankei, the seventeenth-century Japanese Zen master, whom we met when discussing the master–pupil relationship (see pp.118–119), began his search for enlightenment as a child. Writing in later life of his early practice, he recorded that he had pressed himself without mercy, pushing himself to the limits of both mental and physical endurance in search of enlightenment: " ... at times I meditated deep in the mountains, far from human habitation. I made myself primitive shelters out of paper, and ... sat inside in solitary darkness, never lying down. Whenever I heard of a teacher who I thought might be able to help me, I went at once to find him. I lived that way for years." He resolved to meditate to the death, walling himself up in a tiny cell with only a small opening in the wall for food. In his emaciated state he contracted tuberculosis and resigned himself to die, but shortly afterward he had his first enlightenment experience, which left him with the realization that "all things are perfectly resolved in the Unborn". On his deathbed Bankei chided his followers for their tears, and told them, "How do you expect to see me if you look at me in terms of life and death?"

Bankei's "Unborn Zen" – as it came to be known – did much to reform Zen practice, which by his time had become rent by disputes. But, given the impossibility of putting such a concept into words, how can we know more about the nature of this "Unborn"? Master Han Shan, the sixteenth- to seventeenth-century Ch'an master who also practised Pure Land Buddhism, describes his own profound enlightenment experience as follows: " ... body and mind disappeared ... in their place was a great brightness, spherical and full, clear and still as a great mirror containing all the mountains and rivers and the whole Earth ... afterward there was no hindrance in meditation from sounds or forms ... ".

However, Master Hakuin (see p.115) insisted that enlightenment did not lead to a rejection of the world of form. Rather, he believed that it allowed us to see the identification of form with emptiness. The last few lines of one of his poems illustrate this: "Boundless and free is the sky [of enlightenment] / Bright the full moon of wisdom! / Truly, is anything missing now? / Nirvana is right here, before your eyes: / This very place is the Lotus Land, / This very body is the Buddha."

Zen and the Bodhisattva Ideal

Zen belongs to the Mahayana tradition of Buddhism, which means that it recognizes the Bodhisattva Ideal as the perfect symbolic expression of compassion. In Buddhism, the Bodhisattva is a man or woman who has reached the brink of final enlightenment and who could therefore enter Nirvana and leave behind the wheel of birth, death and rebirth, but who voluntarily postpones this consummation of physical existence in order to return, lifetime after lifetime, to help all other sentient beings to enter Nirvana as well.

As an ideal of perfect altruism this is hard to beat. The Bodhisattva has no more to gain for him- or herself. The world has nothing more to offer now that he or she has reached the point of entry into Nirvana. No amount of praise, no reward from fellow men and women is wanted or needed; no personal satisfaction, no feel-good factor is necessary. The decision to return to the physical world and to continue to experience its suffering is taken solely for the benefit of others.

Each day the monks and retreatants in Zen monasteries repeat one of the Bodhisattva vows – to save all sentient beings. The full set of Bodhisattva vows, four in number, is completed by pledges to destroy our passions and desires, to study the Dharma teachings, and

THE CELESTIAL BODHISATTVAS

In addition to those who return to Earth, there are said to be Celestial Bodhisattvas, who help all sentient beings by remaining at more exalted levels of existence. Often these are referred to as Buddhas, and practitioners who wish to go more deeply into Zen may like to study the various levels of Bodhisattvas in more detail. But for present purposes, it is enough to know that certain Bodhisattvas are said to exist in other dimensions, where they continue to honour their vow to save others.

Avalokiteshvara, the Bodhisattva of compassion, is particularly respected in Zen (and in Tibetan Buddhism, in which under the name Chenreizig he is said to reincarnate in successive Dalai Lamas). Other Celestial Bodhisattvas, who are highly regarded by Zen, include Samantabadra, from whose vows all Bodhisattvas are said to arise; Tsitigarbharaj, who helps those who fall into the hell realm; and Amitabha, the Buddha of Boundless Light, who is associated with Pure Land Buddhism (see pp.128–9).

to attain the Buddha-way. Thus – and this is essential to any understanding of Zen – the practitioner follows the Zen path not to gain enlightenment for his or her own benefit, nor to experience *satori* for personal reasons, but in order to be in a position fully to help others. In this way, the "merit" gained through practice is given each day to others. This may sound simplistic, but it is in fact a profound and intensely spiritual teaching. The more the practitioner bears this concept in mind throughout daily life, the more his or her Buddha-nature will reveal itself. It is good to follow the monks' example and repeat the first of the four vows to yourself at the start and finish of each of your meditation sessions: "All beings, however limitless in number, I vow to carry across."

Zen, Amitabha and the Pure Land

For many people it may seem strange that Zen, with its emphasis upon the here and now and upon the practitioner's own efforts, has many affinities with Pure Land Buddhism, which looks to the Celestial Bodhisattva Amitabha for help (see p.127). Yet the more acquainted one becomes with the two paths, the more their similarities are revealed. This is particularly true in the case of Ch'an (Chinese Zen), in which the master may be a teacher of both Zen and Pure Land.

According to Pure Land Buddhism, Amitabha (Amidha in Japanese tradition) is the Buddha of Boundless Light. He rules over the Western Paradise of Sukhavati, a pure land where those who place their trust in him are reborn. In Sukhavati, Amitabha and his attendant Bodhisattvas (such as Kwan Yin, the female embodiment of compassion) help followers to reach final enlightenment and enter into Nirvana, which is easier from Sukhavati than from this world.

Amitabha is also identified with Amitayus, the Buddha of Boundless Life, thus emphasizing his power to bestow both pure realization (boundless light) and the infinite expansion of self (boundless life) to which this realization leads. But why should the "self-power" of Zen have so much in common with the "other power" of Amitabha? Both teach us to see beyond the limited self. In the case of Zen this is accomplished by seeing through the self into our own true nature, and in Pure Land Buddhism by subordinating this self in devotion to Amitabha. Students of Zen regard the Zen tradition as swifter than Pure Land in that the practitioner realizes his or her true nature in this lifetime, whereas those who follow the Pure Land path consider realization arises only after further work in Sukhavati.

THE POWER OF MANTRA MEDITATION

Pure Land practice involves mantra meditation, the repetition of "Praise to Amidha Buddha", which is "*Namu Amidhu Butsu*" in Japanese or "*Nanwu Omito Fo*" in Chinese. It is said that if you repeat this mantra with total devotion only once in your lifetime, you will be reborn in Amitabha's Pure Land. Some Zen practitioners also incorporate mantra meditation, using the words from the *Prajnaparamita* (*Perfection of Wisdom*) text: "*Gatte Gatte Parasamgatte Bodhi Svaha*" ("Gone beyond, gone completely beyond, oh! what an awakening, all hale!"); but here the mantra is regarded as an affirmation of our own essential nature rather than an invocation to a power above the self.

If you wish to use mantra meditation as part of your Zen practice, try using the mantra from the *Prajnaparamita* given here. Focus on your breathing, then repeat the mantra, synchronizing it with each breath. But take care not to repeat the words mindlessly – try to give the mantra your whole attention.

Zen and the Concept of No-self

If nothing has a separate, independent existence, this must also be true of what we call our "self", which differs from situation to situation, from day to day, even from hour to hour. Our moods, our experiences, our physical health, and so on, all influence who we feel ourselves to be at any one time. Looked at closely, the "self" appears to be no more than a collection of fluctuating self-concepts.

Zen invites us to recognize this, and to ask if there is anything behind these self-concepts. We can start by examining the process of thinking. Is the act of thinking self-contained? Or is there a thinker who does the thinking? If there is a thinker, who or what is it? If we label it conscious-ness, does it have to be conscious of something in order to exist?

"... if we turn inward and prove our True-nature – that True-self is no-self, our own Self is no-self – we go beyond ego and past clever words."

Hakuin

Reflecting on such questions may tempt us to conclude that there is no "self" as such, that the concept of self is just a useful construction. This would be fine if life were perfect, but anxieties, setbacks and the inevitability of death mean that for most of us it is anything but ideal. Zen invites us to discover that if we can liberate ourselves from our misguided way of seeing the world, our natural state is free from suf-fering. This is not a woolly claim that everything will be fine if only we can convince ourselves so; it is an invitation to look and decide for our-selves. Thus Zen agrees with Christ's teaching that when the truth is known, "the truth shall make you free" (John 8:32). And knowing the whole truth includes knowing the truth about ourselves.

EXERCISE 25: ASK "WHAT AM I?"

It is said that each koan develops a different aspect of the mind, and that all koans therefore throw light upon the fundamental question "What (or who) am I?", which is in itself a koan. In this exercise we meditate directly upon the concept of "self". By learning more of our inner reality we also find out more about the outer world, as ultimately all phenomena play themselves out within our own minds.

- Sit on your cushion and take up your meditation posture. Centre yourself by focusing upon your breathing for a few minutes.

- When your mind has become uncluttered, introduce the question "What am I?" As with all koans, do not actively wrack your brain for answers. Instead, hold the question in your mind, and examine it, as if it were something novel that you have just discovered.

- If your mind wanders, gently bring it back each time and focus again on the question. Adopt the attitude that the answer – or the resolution – to the koan will come in time, whether now or later.

Joy in the Morning, Sleep at Night – What Else?

There is a saying in Zen: "Joy in the morning, sleep at night – what else?" This expresses Zen in all its simplicity. Life itself is the gift, if we are only wise enough to see it, and to greet it with joy each morning and with sleep each evening. This can seem difficult when we are tired or stressed, and downright impossible if we are struggling with a major life crisis or trying to come to terms with an event such as bereavement. But, little by little, as we go deeper into Zen, our perspective begins to change.

" When an ordinary man gains knowledge, he is a sage; when a sage gains understanding, he is an ordinary man."

Zen saying

It is worth recalling that even the Zen masters experienced enlightenment in stages, rather than in one absolute moment when everything became clear. Sometimes it is when we seem to be making least headway that, like a gift of grace, we catch a glimpse of ultimate clarity. This is particularly true if we look at the reasons for our apparent lack of progress. Why are we stuck? Why have we appeared to slip back?

One of the many remarkable things about advanced Zen practitioners is their calmness in the face of the challenges life has to offer. This does not make them indifferent to pain and suffering in others – compassion for those in need and for those experiencing misfortune is one of the cornerstones of Zen. In their own lives Zen practitioners see beyond the ever-changing, illusory nature of physical phenomena, but they recognize that

not everyone can share with them this insight. For most people compassion means not lessons in spiritual philosophy but practical help, support and guidance. However, Zen practitioners have come to realize that life itself is the ultimate koan. Who are we? Why are we here? Where are we going? Once we begin to penetrate this koan, we can see that life carries meaning, and is not limited to the world of outer appearances.

Having seen into the essence from which the outer world arises and of which it is an expression, the Zen master is not distressed by past disappointments nor troubled by future anxieties. The moment-by-moment experience of existence, rather than goals such as wealth, power and prestige with which we clutter existence, is our only real teacher. It is the way in which we respond to life, and not the business of living, that distresses us. Once we free our minds from this self-inflicted suffering, we can come closer to what life, in its fullness and completeness, its difficulties and obstacles, is trying to tell us.

Remember the traditional Zen qualities of Great Faith, Great Courage and Great Inquiry, which we first encountered at the beginning of this book (see pp.22-3). Zen asks us to work with great faith that there is a resolution to life's koan, with great courage to experience this resolution, and with determination to continue our great enquiry until we do so.

However, no matter how hard we try to keep up our practice, there will inevitably come a time when we feel a need for encouragement – the reassurance that we are making progress. We may even seek an objective test of some kind that assesses how well we are doing with our practice. (In the West the idea of measuring progress by scores, grades and qualifications is impressed upon us at an early age.) Alas, Zen meditation is not that kind of exercise. A Zen master will only listen to what we have to say about our practice and advise us on our difficulties; there is no question of passing judgment. If we have successfully resolved a koan, he or she will indicate this, but this indication will be as enigmatic as the koan itself.

Ultimately, Zen teaches us that we are each the resolution of our own koan. As the favourite symbol for the Zen journey – the circle – denotes, koan and resolution are one and the same, and that for which we are searching is the very thing engaged in the search.

EXERCISE 26:
FIND THE ANSWER TO YOURSELF

Whenever you sit in meditation you are making "progress" (but
remember that sitting lost in thought is not meditation). Aid
your self-exploration by asking yourself the following questions.

- Is your mind less likely to wander during meditation now than when
  you began to practise (ignoring day-to-day fluctuations)? How are
  you now more attentive and less forgetful?

- Are you generally more mindful of the present, and less inclined to
  dwell on memories of the past or ponder the future? How are you
  more aware of the interplay – and interdependency – of form and
  emptiness in daily life?

- Are you more aware of your interconnectedness with nature? Do you
  now take more pleasure in the natural world? If so, in what ways?
  And do you now have more empathy with other people? Have you
  become more tolerant and compassionate? If so, how?

- Would you say that you are more at peace with yourself? Are you
  aware of "not knowing" the "self"? How are you more appreciative
  of the gift of life?

CHAPTER 6

THE JOURNEY IN PICTURES

With its love of nature and of paintings, and its distrust of over-reliance upon language, Zen not surprisingly makes good use of pictures as teaching devices.

In this chapter we explore the best-known set of Zen images – the bull- or ox-herding pictures, which are a sequence of ten drawings by the twelfth-century Chinese Zen master Kakuan. The pictures tell the story of a young boy's attempt to locate and capture an ox. Copied and elaborated upon many times by various artists over the centuries, the ox-herding pictures remain one of the best ways of understanding Zen.

Under each drawing Master Kakuan wrote comments in verse and prose (always from the viewpoint of the young boy), intended to supplement the images rather than to explain what is happening in them. Every picture is an object of contemplation in itself, revealing deeper levels of meaning the more we reflect upon it.

Setting Off

Before beginning to work with the ox-herding pictures, it is helpful to remember that in Kakuan's time the ox was the most common and useful domesticated animal in China – the perfect symbol for our true nature, which is everywhere around us and deep within our own being. In the first seven pictures, the "seeker" is shown as a young boy, who represents our own unenlightened self: naïve, unrealized, and yet impelled by an innate longing to be united with our own true nature.

The ten pictures are a record of spiritual development, an account of a journey from ignorance to wisdom and to that which lies beyond both. They are an inspired teaching device and are as relevant to our own spiritual journey today as they were when Kakuan created them.

The ox-herding pictures are extraordinarily friendly, and give us a wonderful sense of being taken by the hand. They make us feel that our frailties are understood, our determination is applauded and the outcome of our search is assured. Across eight centuries and more, Master Kakuan is still with us, his insights are our insights, and his compassion for the innocent child who begins the search is our compassion for ourselves.

Look through each of the pictures before you start using them in your practice. Try to recreate them in your mind, so that you can visualize them in meditation and at other times. Do not be over-concerned with the words written about them – these are only hints and whispers. The pictures belong to you, as they do to everyone who chooses to work with them, and if you wish you can write your own words to them, always taking – as Kakuan did – the role of the young boy.

1. THE SEARCH FOR THE OX

Kakuan's verse tells us that he endlessly searches for the ox "following unnamed rivers, lost upon the winding pathways of distant mountains". But the ox is not to be found, and with his strength exhausted the boy hears only "the locusts chirping through the forest at night". In his prose commentary, Kakuan asks himself why he is driven to find the ox, and answers that it is "because of separation from my true nature". The search leads him far from home (far from known, familiar ways of thinking), and he is unsure which of the many possible pathways to take. His own "greed and fear", and the dualistic world of "good and bad" (the chirping of locusts), entangle him in the darkness of his own ignorance.

The first ox-herding picture shows us our own predicament. We long to find our true nature, to escape from the darkness around us, but we are confused by the many pathways – the many different theories, ideas and teachings – that confront us. Yet this first picture, like the rest of the sequence, is a symbol of hope and optimism, not of despair. We already have the priceless gift of belief that our true nature exists (the Great Faith of Zen), that enlightenment is real, and that we should begin the search.

2. DISCOVERING THE FOOTPRINTS

In the second picture, Kakuan tells us that he comes across the footprints of the ox "along the riverbank ... and under the scented grass". This allows him to know which path to follow. Suddenly, possibilities open up in front of him. He has the reward now of knowing that the ox exists, instead of only believing that it does. If he fails to follow the footprints, he has simply himself to blame. It is now the ox itself – his own true nature – that is showing him the way.

For Kakuan, the footprints were the Buddhist sutras, and it was these sutras that allowed him to find, among the many different teachings available to him, the one that would lead him to the ox. The Zen method is there in the sutras, but it is also to be found in all the great traditions, provided we look below the surface – symbolized here by Kakuan's reference to the footprints of the ox revealing themselves "below the scented grass". We must look beyond the mere surface teachings, deeper than the words of others.

3. PERCEIVING THE OX

Now Kakuan is able actually to catch sight of the ox. His verse tells us that the ox cannot hide "from the nightingale's song, from the warmth of the sun, from the gentle touch of the wind", from the shades of green that fill the natural world and express themselves in "the willows along the river bank". Now that the ox is in sight, he has more than just its footprints to guide him, he has the animal itself – "the gate is entered ... the smallest thing is not separate from itself".

Thus we learn that the first glimpse of the ox comes when all our senses are opened up to nature. The song of the nightingale, the warm sunshine, the wind, the rain and the colours that surround and embrace us, are all expressions of our true nature. Nothing is separate from or isolated from this one true nature. There is no distinction between what we are and what we experience.

Now try the exercise on the following page.

EXERCISE 27:
UNDERSTAND YOUR OWN SEARCH

You can allow the pictures to communicate with you in their (and your) own way, but you may find the following exercise a useful guide as to how to approach the first three images.

- Think about the young boy. Remember that he represents you, exactly as you are now. He has Great Faith (see pp.22–3) that the ox exists. You may wish to contemplate the first three pictures and examine your own Great Faith (even if you would not describe it in such emphatic terms). How did this "faith" arise? Did it come intuitively, or is it a result of your studies, or did it stem from another source?

- Ask yourself what prompts your longing to find the ox. Is it a wish to grasp something for yourself? Or is it a desire to satisfy your curiosity? Is it a way to escape from the pressures and sheer ordinariness of daily life? Or is it perhaps a feeling that finding the ox is the reason for your existence? What form does your longing take? And when you first see the footprints of the ox, what is the scented grass that may obscure them?

- You may wish to think about the pathways that you have already trodden in your life, some of which you may have followed for a greater or lesser time than Zen. Think about why they failed to lead you to the ox. Did you abandon them too soon? Did they appear to lead nowhere?

- The first glimpse of the ox seems to depend upon opening all the senses to what is happening around you, and in particular to the natural world. What prevents this "opening" in everyday life? What has happened in your life to close down some of the channels of communication between you and the creative reality that expresses itself through all living things?

4. CATCHING THE OX

Kakuan tells us in his verse that he "seizes the ox with a great struggle", but new difficulties arise. The ox struggles to free itself with "inexhaustible will and power", galloping away "to the high plateau far above the cloud mists", or plunging down into "impenetrable ravines". The only way to control it seems to be through the use of greater force.

In his prose commentary, Kakuan ascribes the waywardness of the ox to its "infatuation with other scenery and for sweeter grass", and to its "stubborn and untamed mind". His first experience of true spirituality leads him to mistake enlightenment as an achievement of his own ego and he is in danger of being led "to the high plateau" of false spiritual exaltation. Alternatively, his fear that he is losing hold of the ox gives him the impression that it is taking him down into "an impenetrable ravine" (the darkness reported by many mystics when they feel divine vision has forsaken them). The "stubborn and untamed mind" of the ox is not only the elusiveness of our true nature, but the waywardness of our own ego, which seeks to impose itself even upon experiences of enlightenment.

5. TAMING THE OX

Self-discipline – "the whip and the rope" in the words of Kakuan – are
necessary to prevent the ox from straying away "down some dusty road".
But once the ox is tamed, it "becomes naturally gentle", and can be
unfettered once more. The commentary explains that it is our train of
thoughts that leads us astray. If we start with a deluded thought, we will
be taken increasingly further from the truth. But when the "first thought
arises from enlightenment", all those that follow are true. Delusion comes
from subjectivity, not objectivity. It is only our own mind that misleads us.

This shows us clearly how the mind, once it begins to experience the
enlightened state, can still produce distortions if it retains the deluded
notion that this state has anything to do with the individual ego. Only if
our initial thought arises directly from the enlightened state itself, rather
than from concepts about it, will our thoughts and actions remain true.
Once we recognize this we will act freely and spontaneously from
compassion rather than from the contrived meanderings and obscurities
of the subjective self.

6. RIDING THE OX HOME

The identification between the ox and the boy is achieved. Kakuan's verse puts it that, on the back of the ox, "slowly I return homeward; the sound of my flute floats through the evening ... . Whoever hears the melody will join me." The prose commentary adds that "gain and loss are assimilated; I sing the same song as the village woodman, and play the tunes of the children ... no-one can call me back".

The opposites of "gain and loss", of true nature and self-nature, have disappeared. There is only the sound of the single flute (the sound of the "one hand" that we heard when discussing koans), and it is the sound of the natural world (the woodman) and of the pure mind (symbolized by the child). All who "hear" the melody of the flute – all who open their senses to the truth expressed by reality itself – can share the experience of riding on the ox. There is now no slipping back, no diversion into "high plateaux", "impenetrable ravines" or "dusty roads". There is only clarity, and the tranquillity of the slow ride homeward.

Now try the exercise on the following page.   145

EXERCISE 28:
GRASP YOUR TRUE NATURE

Pictures 4–6 take us through the resolution of the search. Try the
following exercise to help you grasp what it is to catch, tame and at
last feel in harmony with the ox – your own true nature.

- Ask yourself what motivates you to struggle with the ox. The
  battle is essentially with yourself, so are you struggling against
  the misconceptions that you bring to the search, the distractions
  of the outside world, or the delusions of your own mind?

- Try to explore the deluded thoughts that still threaten to lead you
  astray after the first glimpse of enlightenment. (You may not yet
  have had this glimpse, but your delusions are always with you, and
  even now you can begin to examine them and lay them aside.)

- Imagine what life would be like "beyond gain and loss". The world
  would still present itself as it does now, but you would recognize the
  interdependency of all things. The separation between yourself and
  your true nature would also disappear. How would you experience
  such a world without opposites?

7. THE OX TRANSCENDED

The seventh picture shows the boy no longer on the ox, but sitting peacefully outside his simple dwelling, enjoying the dawn and the beauty around him. Some may find this picture difficult to understand. Having caught the ox and ridden it home, why has the boy now seemingly abandoned it? Kakuan puts it that "the ox too can rest"; its task is done – the ox was only a symbol, and symbols are now no longer necessary.

Whatever symbols we choose from our various spiritual traditions can be laid aside once we are in contact with reality itself. To hang on to these representations is to mistake their purpose. It is worth recalling the Zen saying that we should be guided by the finger pointing at the moon, but we should never mistake it for the moon itself (see p.14). In other words, we must stop looking at the finger, and look to where it is pointing. The ox has taken the boy home, and it is now superfluous.

The "thatched hut" that is home emphasizes again the importance of simplicity, as does the posture of the boy, sitting quietly watching the dawn, which has replaced the darkness of delusion.

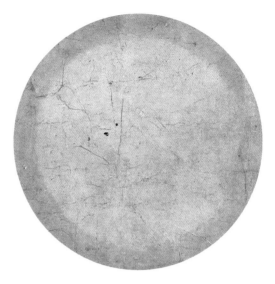

8. BOTH OX AND SELF TRANSCENDED

An empty circle is complete in and of itself. With no beginning and no end, it is defined by the space contained within it and by the outer space which in turn contains it. Space and form are both aspects of the circle. Completeness has now been obtained, and the self is seen as just as much of a symbol as the ox. Both boy and ox have led us to this completeness, and the boy can share the same rest as the ox. "All merge in no-thing," says Kakuan, "Heaven is so vast no message can stain it."

Kakuan now "seeks no state of enlightenment" and "does not remain where no enlightenment exists". Concepts like "enlightenment" cannot contain the reality of the heavens, and are seen in turn merely as symbols. Heaven is beyond limitations, so no "message" (no description) can truly "stain" (represent) it. And because ultimate reality unites all things and is beyond concepts, it is literally "no-thing". There are now no limitations upon mind – it is both the form and the emptiness of the circle. And as this state is not identified with the individual ego, there is no risk that the praise and adulation of the world will be taken personally.

9. REACHING THE SOURCE

In the ninth picture, form reappears, but there is no sign of the boy or the ox. Form exists in and of itself. The natural world is as it is and as it has always been. In reality there was no need to go journeying in order to find our true nature. It was here all the time, arising in each moment of existence, presenting us continually with the answer to the koan of our own identity. "Better to have been blind and deaf from the beginning," comments Kakuan.

The mind is now free from attachment, even to itself. There is no need to grasp at anything, even at the ox, for we are already our own true nature, and provided that we do not overlay it with concepts and false notions about reality, then we can abide in this nature from the beginning.

10. INTO THE WORLD

The young boy is now an old sage. With a round belly that symbolizes the fullness of experience, he returns to the market-place to share whatever he has with others. He carries the staff of true purpose, and the wine jug of true desire, which he offers to the small boy who comes to meet him. Sage and small boy are not opposites but aspects of the one reality.

Kakuan goes on to say: "the trees before me are alive". Life is all around us and flowing through us, and we can never be separated from it. Thus we need not fear death, which is only the end of our existence when seen from the perspective of the ever-changing world of form.

The final sentence of Kakuan's prose commentary is a reminder to us of the use that the Zen master makes of the word "I". Kakuan says, "I visit the wine shop and the market, and everyone I look upon becomes enlightened." So has Kakuan returned to the world of the ego? Decidedly not – "I" now represents his true nature, which is one with the true nature of everyone else. All that has happened is that he has realized what he has always been, and now offers this realization to others.

Now try the exercise on the opposite page.

EXERCISE 29: ASSESS YOUR PROGRESS

In Picture 10, the enlightened sage goes to the market-place to teach others. While you may feel that you have a way to go on your personal journey, this exercise can help you gauge how far you have reached (but do not regard it as a final assessment of your progress).

• Reflect upon how your practice has altered the way you *are* in the world. Do you feel that you now participate more in life, rather than feel divorced from it? You may feel that the changes are relatively slight. Or you may think you that you fluctuate, some days being influenced by Zen, at others slipping back into old ways. But remember that the important thing is that you have entered the path.

• Assess your development by dividing it into different areas, such as relationships with other people and relationships with objects and events. Ask yourself whether you are now more aware of the interconnectedness of all things. Are you better able to keep your attention focused on the task in hand? Are you more patient and understanding toward family, friends and colleagues? Are you more tranquil in the face of difficulties and setbacks, and more effective in dealing with them?

Conclusion

As we have stressed throughout this book, Zen is a particular state of mind, which is attained through Zen meditation. It then becomes a part of our daily lives, influencing the way in which we see the world and ourselves: permeating garden design, the use of space, flower arranging, painting and poetry; and leading to an attitude of simplicity and compassion as we face the challenges in life.

No-one who studies Zen in any depth can help but be changed by it. Although firmly located within Buddhism, the Zen state of mind is a feature of all the great spiritual traditions, and we can profit from Zen without abandoning our preferred tradition. Essentially, Zen training provides us with a wise friend who is always with us – humorous, gentle and compassionate when we need humour, gentleness and compassion; stern and directive when we need sternness and direction. Zen asks us to see things as they really are, instead of living our lives in a kind of waking daydream, clouded by illusion about reality and our own nature.

It is appropriate to end this book with a brief description of the meditation state known as "silent illumination" – one of the most venerated practices in Soto Zen – as it illustrates the state of mind reached by the advanced meditator, usually after many years of dedicated practice. Generally, the master recommends silent illumination only after the meditator has gained proficiency in working with the breath or with koans, as the practice consists essentially of meditating upon silence itself. In this state, the mind is said to reflect everything, like a clear, calm pool, and time has no limits. Zen teaches that when the mind has experienced this illumination, the whole cosmos can be seen in a grain of sand. In the following poem, Ch'an (Chinese Zen) master Hung Chih Cheng-Chueh (11th–12th century) gives us a fleeting insight into the experience of the mind when it reaches this profound state of illumination – more evocative in a few lines than any lengthy explanation:

> "*Full of wonder is the pure illumination.*
> *The moon's appearance, a river of stars.*
> *Snow-clad pines, clouds hovering on mountain peaks,*
> *In darkness, they glow with brightness.*
> *In shadows, they shine with a splendid light,*
> *Like the dreaming of a crane flying in empty space,*
> *Like the clear, still water of an autumn pool.*
> *Endless eons dissolve into nothingness,*
> *Each indistinguishable from the other.*
> *In this illumination all striving is forgotten.*"

Nothing needs to be added to this description. Whether we reach this state or not is less important than the fact that the human mind is not only capable of attaining it, but also able to recognize this state as its natural way of being. Reading Hung Chih Cheng-Chueh's serene words enables us to see the true beauty of the tradition that he represented – a tradition that was handed down from the Buddha himself, and that has retained its potency through countless generations.

However, should we allow ourselves to become too carried away, the Zen master will tell us sternly to stop losing ourselves in fantasy, and to go and sit on our cushions and continue our practice.

Glossary

Bodhidharma The first Zen patriarch, probably born in Ceylon in the 6th century BCE. Credited with bringing Zen to China.

Bodhisattva An enlightened being, who is said to hold back from entering Nirvana (and thus from becoming a fully-realized Buddha) until the rest of creation can also enter.

Buddha "The Fully Awakened One". The historical Buddha, Buddha Shakyamuni, was born *c*.560BCE.

Dogen (1200–1253) The Japanese founder of Soto Zen.

dokusan The private interview between pupil and Master.

enlightenment Freedom from limitations of the mind, and the expansion of awareness until it realizes unity with the One Mind (and with all things).

Hekiganroku "The Blue Cliff Record". A collection of 100 Zen koans.

kensho The first experience of *satori* or enlightenment.

kin-hin Walking meditation. Usually practised in between periods of sitting meditation during the Zen *sesshin*.

koan A paradoxical statement or question resolved only through an awakening of deeper levels of spirit. Used mainly in Rinzai Zen.

kyosaku The flat stick carried by the head monk (or his deputy), used to strike the shoulders of those distracted or experiencing drowsiness during meditation.

mondo Short question and answer dialogues between the master and pupil.

Mumonkan The "Gateless Gate". Along with the *Hegikanroku*, the *Mumonkan* is one of the best-known collections of koans.

Rinzai (Chinese *Linchi*) One of the two main schools of Zen Buddhism (see also *Soto*); founded in Japan by the monk Eisei (1141–1215). Both the *koan* and the *mondo* are used extensively.

satori The state of consciousness beyond duality and discrimination. The enlightenment experience.

sesshin A retreat involving intensive Zen practice under a master.

Soto (Chinese *Tsaotung*) One of the two main schools of Zen Buddhism (see also *Rinzai*); established in Japan by the monk Dogen (1200–1253). Emphasizes the importance of *zazen*.

zazen Literally "Zen sitting". Also used generally to describe the postures and breathing techniques used in Zen while in the sitting position.

Further Reading

Bancroft, A. *Zen: Direct Pointing at Reality*, Thames & Hudson (London), 1979

Cleary, T. *No Barrier: Unlocking the Zen Koan*, HarperCollins (London and New York), 1993

Dumoulin, H. (transl. J. Maraldo) *Zen Enlightenment: Origins and Meaning*, Weatherhill (New York and Tokyo), 1979

Enomoya-Lassalle, H. (transl. Michelle Bromley) *The Practice of Zen Meditation*, Aquarian Press (Wellingborough, UK), 1990

Goddard, D., ed. *A Buddhist Bible*, Beacon Press (Boston), 1994

Hass, R. *The Essential Haiku: Versions of Basho, Buson and Isso*, Ecco Press (Hopewell, New Jersey), 1994

Herrigel, E. (transl. R. F. C. Hull) *Zen in the Art of Archery*, Routledge & Kegan Paul (London), 1972 and Random House (New York), 1999

Herrigel, G. (trans R. F. C. Hull) *Zen in the Art of Flower Arrangement*, Routledge & Kegan Paul (London), 1974

Kapleau, P. *The Three Pillars of Zen: Teaching, Practice and Enlightenment*, Rider (London), 1980

Kennett, J. *Selling Water by the River: A Manual of Zen Training*, Random House (New York), 1972

Linssen, R. (transl. D. Abrahams-Curiel) *Living Zen*, Grove Press (New York), 1958

Long, J. *How to Paint the Chinese Way*, Blandford Books (Dorset, UK) and Sterling Books (New York), 1983

Reps, P. *Zen Flesh, Zen Bones*, Penguin Books (Harmondsworth, UK), 1957 and Charles E. Tuttle (Rutland, Vermont and Tokyo), 1998

Schloegel, I. *The Zen Way*, Sheldon Press (London), 1977

Sekida, K. *Two Zen Classics: Mumonkan and Hekiganroku*, Weatherhill (New York and Tokyo), 1977

Suzuki, S. *Zen Mind, Beginner's Mind*, Weatherhill (New York and Tokyo), 1970

Wood, E. *Zen Dictionary*, Penguin (Harmondsworth, UK), 1977

Zen Master Enji Zenji (transl. Yoko Okuda) *Discourse on the Inexhaustible Lamp*, The Zen Centre (London), 1989

Zen Master Seung Sahn *Dropping Ashes on the Buddha*, Grove Press (New York), 1976

Zen Centres

UK
Buddhist Society, 58 Eccleston Square,
London SW1V 1PH
tel: 020 7824 5858

Kanzeon Sangha, Top Cottage,
Parsonage Farm West, Uffculme,
Devon EX15 3DR
tel: 01884 841026

Reading Buddhist Priory,
176 Cressingham Road, Reading,
Berkshire RG2 7LW
tel: 0118 9860750

Throssel Hole Buddhist Abbey,
Carrshield, Hexham, Northumberland
NE47 8AL tel: 01434 345204

USA
Cambridge Buddhist Association,
75 Sparks Street, Cambridge MA 02138
tel: 617 4918857

Community of Mindful Living,
PO Box 7355, Berkeley, CA 94707
tel: 510 527351

Diamond Sangha, 2119 Kaloa Way,
Honolulu HI 96822 tel: 808 9460666

Kanzeon Zen Center of Utah,
1274 East South Temple, Salt Lake
City, UT 84102 tel: 801 3288414

Providence Zen Center (Diamond Hill
Monastery), 99 Pond Rd, Cumberland
RI 02864 2726 tel: 401 6581464

Rochester Zen Center, 7 Arnold Park,
Rochester, NY 14607 tel: 716 4739180

San Francisco Zen Center, 300 Page St,
CA 94102 tel: 415 8633136

Shasta Abbey, 3612 Summit Drive,
Mount Shasta, CA 96067
tel: 916 9264208

Springwater Center, 7179 Springwater,
NY 14560 tel: 716 6692142

Zen Center of Los Angeles, 923 South
Normandie Ave, Los Angeles,
CA 90006–1301 tel: 213 3872351

Zen Community of New York,
21 Park Ave, Yonkers, NY 10703
tel: 914 3769000

CANADA
Zen Buddhist Temple, 86 Vaughan Rd,
Toronto ON M6C 2M1 tel: 416 6580137

Zen Center of Vancouver, 4269 Brant
St, Vancouver BC V5N 5B5
tel: 604 8790229

AUSTRALIA
Sydney Zen Centre, 251 Young St,
Annandale, New South Wales 2038
tel: 02 96602993

Zen Group of Western Australia,
29 Claremont Crescent, Claremont,
Western Australia 6010
tel: 09 3856026

Index

Acknowledgments

Ox-herding pictures –
Shokuku-ji Temple, Kyoto,
Japan, courtesy of the Kyoto
National Museum, Japan.